Bringing Up Boys with Tom

Published by
Shoal Creek Studios
shefelmanbooks.com

Cover Design by: Heidi Dorey and Janice Shefelman
Editor-in-Chief: Mindy Reed
Interior Design by: Danielle H. Acee, authorsassistant.com

ISBN: 978-0-578-69015-5 Hardcover
Cataloging-in-Publication Data
Shefelman, Janice
Bringing Up Boys with Tom/Janice Shefelman
p. cm.
Library of Congress Control Number: 2020912592

First edition 2020.

Bringing Up Boys
with Tom

A Memoir

Janice Shefelman

To Tom
my forever love
and Father of our boys
Karl and Daniel

Contents

Dear Reader,

I promised Tom that I would write our memoir if he wrote one about his childhood and youth. He did. He called it *My Youth and Art.* Now I am keeping my promise.

Bringing Up Boys with Tom begins with Tom's and my life together after returning from our journey around the world as told in *Honeymoon Hobos.* Much of bringing up children is by example. Thus I will tell about Tom's and my activities as well, for whatever influence they had on Karl and Daniel.

When Tom asked me to marry him, I smiled and said, "Yes, if I don't have to cook or have children." I am still lukewarm about cooking but bringing up our boys was one of the greatest joys of my life.

Janice Shefelman

1

What Now?

*W*hat could possibly follow a yearlong journey around the world? Simple. Tom's and my first home together, friendships to renew, stories to tell, a boat to sail, dreams to pursue, and boys to bring up.

We returned to Austin in June, 1955, and found a spacious apartment above a three-car garage on Enfield Road, high above the Shoal Creek greenbelt. We had a screened porch entry to a sunny living room, bedroom, complete kitchen and a dining room.

I loved the central location because we could walk to the grocery store, Kash-Karry on 12th Street, and to the Drag. At night, after dinner, Tom and I sometimes walked to the Night Hawk restaurant on Guadalupe for dessert, even in the coldest weather. Our favorite was warm apple pie with vanilla ice cream. If we had dinner there it was invariably their famous chopped steak and baked potato.

It was our place, the place where Tom proposed to me with a diamond engagement ring around the queen in a traveling chess set. Only Tom would think of doing that.

How could I refuse? He had the hands of a laborer, the body of an athlete, the face of an artist, and a childlike sense of humor. The combination fascinated me.

Now we were back among friends who welcomed us and at least pretended to want to hear about our travels. Seymour and Barbie Fogel invited us to dinner in their home and studio they called Southwind.

"I'm cooking a pot of beans," Barbie said on the phone. "We'd love to see you and hear your stories. And Sy has some new paintings to show."

Sy was a professor in the Department of Art at the University of Texas. Tom had succeeded in getting a commission for him to paint a colorful thirty-foot geometric mural in the American National Bank, which Tom designed when he worked for Kuehne, Brooks & Barr before we married. Partner Max Brooks considered Tom his golden boy and gave him design freedom.

When the construction was finished, Tom took me to the bank's opening party as his betrothed. I was dazzled by the architecture and all the praise Tom received that night, including from the bank president, Eddie Wroe, who helped finance our trip around the world and remained a good friend ever after.

In gratitude for the commission, Sy made an oil painting for us as a wedding gift that he called "Much Happiness," but I named it "Tall Ship at Sea" for the blue-green color and abstract shapes.

Tom and I eagerly accepted Barbie's invitation. She loved to cook and it showed in her ample figure. Sy, a handsome, rugged man with dark, curly hair and intense eyes, worked relentlessly and passionately in his spacious home studio. I sensed that the two of them had a vital love life.

That night, full of beans and travel stories, we adjourned to Sy's studio to see his work in progress. It was a large blue-on-blue abstract painting. Delicate black figures with round heads swam about in the blue.

"Interesting, Sy." That is what Tom always said when he did not know what to say.

"What do you call it?" I asked.

"Icarian Flight, for Icarus who, like me, was foolhardy and daring."

We laughed. What I loved about Sy and learned from him was his boldness, which can get you in trouble like Icarus or get what you want.

As for pursuing our dreams, Tom had a job waiting for him at Fehr & Granger Architects. Both partners had great respect for Tom's design ability. Before we left on our journey, they offered him a position upon our return in a year.

I wanted to continue teaching in elementary school as I had in Dallas before we married, preferably the fourth grade, my favorite age group. They are independent readers with open minds and still relate to adults as well as their peers.

I applied to the Austin Independent School District, but before an offer came, our dear friends, Clark and Charlotte Craig, recommended me to teach third grade at St. Andrew's Episcopal School in central Austin. Clark was an architectural engineer who had worked on several projects with Tom before we married. It was no coincidence that his older daughter, Phoebe, was a third-grader there. A private school with small classes appealed to me, and it was within walking distance of our apartment.

The headmistress and first-grade teacher, Mignon Henry, interviewed me. A tall, thin, no-nonsense woman, she asked me why I wanted to teach at St. Andrew's.

"I like the idea of having the time to relate one on one with children in a small classroom," I said. "And I like the idea that they have educated parents who have given them a rich background that I can build upon."

She smiled. "Yes, with your experience of traveling the world, and with the impressive description of you and Tom that Clark gave me, I think you have much to offer our children."

"Thank you, Mignon, and with you as an inspiration, I will grow as a teacher." I meant it. She was a master.

My third-grade class had only thirteen students. I made home visits and felt supported by the parents. Even so, as for any teacher or student, I was extremely nervous on the first day. Pat Fatter, mother of Mervin who was known as something of a discipline problem, gave me some advice.

"Be firm with Mervin from the very beginning and he'll realize who's in charge."

Gulp.

Sure enough, when my third-graders arrived on that first day, Mervin started running around the room. I took him firmly by the arm and said, "No running, Mervin." It worked.

Phoebe Craig was an ideal student, bright, diligent, and involved. Naturally she was a favorite. I had another, Tibaut Bowman, brightest, most engaged boy in my class. I could count on him to ask and answer questions. Like John Henry from my Dallas fourth grade class, he sucked up knowledge. Though something of a showoff, he was entirely lovable. We knew and loved his parents, Bob and Mary Ann Bowman. Bob was Tom's and my insurance agent.

One day Bob called me to express a concern about Tibaut. "He's very bright but has no direction for using his intelligence. Do you have any suggestions?"

"Yes, Bob, I do. I'm a great believer in children having models, either live ones or book ones, like biographies of people who made a difference in the world."

Bob liked the idea, and I recommended some books for young readers. Years later, when that class had a reunion and invited me, I told Tibaut about my discussion with his dad.

He laughed. "Oh, that explains why I was suddenly flooded with books about famous people."

At that reunion, Tibaut took my hand and said, "You know, I was in love with you in the third and fourth grades."

I nodded. "And you were my favorite little boy — such a smart aleck."

Fortunately, at the end of that year, parents requested that I take my class on to the fourth grade. And Mignon agreed. I felt honored that they thought I had done a good job, and pleased since I already knew the students so well.

As a teacher, and elsewhere, I like to have control and am uncomfortable without it. My class got the idea from the beginning. Perhaps I was too controlling. I can remember a fourth-grade Christmas party when several mothers came to help.

"They're so quiet," David Smith's mother said.

I felt a little guilty and from then on attempted to loosen up a bit.

Christmas at St. Andrew's

Weather permitting, I walked to school, down Enfield Road, across Lamar, and along 12th Street to Pearl, where the school was located in an old two-story house on a spacious property with an annex in back for the fourth- and fifth-grade classes.

Even though all my students were from affluent backgrounds, their abilities varied as much as any class. Rod Arend, teased for being over-weight, had a reading disability. Though at the time, dyslexia was not widely known, I sensed that a reading specialist could help him. I suggested to Helen, his mother, that we take Rod to see a University of Texas professor in the education department.

After examining him, the professor said, "He suffers from dyslexia. That means he reverses the letters in words, but I can help him overcome it."

"Oh, what a relief," Helen said. "What must we do?"

"Bring Rod to me once a week for an hour."

Helen and I did just that, and Rod's ability to read improved. She was so appreciative of my advice that we remained friends after I left St. Andrew's at the end of that year. And she even commissioned Tom to design a new home for her family.

I am proud that both Tom and I could make a difference in the Arend family. Even now I occasionally see Rod around town, especially when Tom and I were regulars for Saturday morning breakfast at Sweetish Hill. Rod grew tall and thin and became a successful real estate salesman.

Phoebe Craig was one of the brightest, most diligent students, though quiet. Perhaps she was extra sensitive to my need for order in the classroom. But when she got out on the playground, she could match or surpass the boys at running, kicking the ball, or jumping rope — a real tomboy. Once I got inspired to jump rope with Phoebe and reinjured my knee where I had torn the cartilage while playing basketball in college intramurals. Later, soon after Karl was born, I went to Dallas to have the torn piece removed. At the hospital I saw a man who had to have his leg cut off at the knee and worried that it was a bad omen for me. Mother took care of Karl, and the doctor made sure I did not lose my leg, only the torn cartilage.

Tom and I often had dinner with Phoebe's parents, Clark and Charlotte, at their house in Tarrytown. Phoebe liked to hang around us until bedtime.

Once, when Charlotte was trying to get her to take a bath, she said, "Phoebe, Janice thinks you have such pretty hair, and now it's time to wash it."

"Then you can come give us a goodnight hug," I added.

She gave me a sweet smile and went off with Charlotte. Afterward, Phoebe and little sister Lucy returned in their nighties, smelling like lavender soap.

Gwen Johnson, another of my favorites, was almost scarily smart but never a showoff. I am not sure whether I taught her anything she did not already know, but at our reunion she told me, "You were the best teacher I ever had."

I find that hard to believe because teaching was not my calling. But I do know that I gave them some valuable experiences.

Each day after lunch I indulged my passion for children's books and read to my class, everything from *Just So Stories* to *Dr. Dolittle* to *Johnny Tremain* to *Charlotte's Web* and more. I also brought classical music recordings, such as "Scheherazade," to play as the children used crayons to draw whatever the music said to them.

I had to force myself to teach science, but geography — ah, there was my inspiration. Using slides from our travels around the world, I loved expanding my students' horizons, hoping to make world citizens out of them.

Since St. Andrew's was an Episcopal school, we had regular chapel. Ministers from different churches came on a rotating basis to lead the services. My favorite was Scotfield Bailey from All Saints. Tall and lean in his black robe, he related to the children in an easygoing way and with a sense of humor that made his eyes lively. The children loved him and flocked to him after chapel was over. My least favorite was Charles Sumners from St. David's, a portly man whose stomach protruded under his robe. He looked down on us and spoke to the children as if he were God. Tom had been a member of his church at one time but left. More on that later.

On weekends, Tom and I took the Snipe out for a sail on Lake Travis. Clark Craig had kept it in his garage while we traveled, broken mast and all. Another friend, Don Marsh, offered to repair the mast for the use of the boat. So when we returned, the Snipe was ready to go.

Now for Tom's return to practicing architecture with Fehr & Granger, a firm known for excellence in modern design. Would he be the "golden boy" that he was at Kuehne, Brooks, & Barr?

2

Beware the Boomerang

*F*ehr & Granger's office was on East 5th Street across from the O. Henry Museum. Two old stone buildings enclosed an entrance courtyard, one housed a Mexican restaurant, the other was full of construction junk. An outdoor staircase led to the second floor office.

The firm had fourteen architects and one lovable secretary, Becky, who managed everything. Charley Granger, the younger partner, had worked for Eero Saarinen and considered himself the design master in the firm. Arthur Fehr was more of a promoter, but each had his own projects. The people in the firm were like a big family, and, along with their spouses, were mothered by Mary Jane Fehr.

One night we invited Charley and his wife Marty to our garage apartment for dinner. The four of us sat on floor cushions around our living room coffee table. Charley was a big, good-looking guy with dark, curly hair who dwarfed his short, slender wife.

"A tribute to Japan, I see," Charley said, looking a bit awkward at the low table.

Tom put his palms together and dipped his head. *"Hai, wakari-mashita."* He loved using the phrases we learned while in Japan and never forgot them because of continued use.

With an amused look on his face, Charley said, "Have you gone native on us?"

Tom grinned. *"Hai, wakarimashita.* It means yes, certainly. And then you say, *Ah so-o-o desu ka,* meaning, is that right?"

Being a good sport, Charley mimicked Tom's gestures and words.

If only I had bought Japanese food. Instead I bought four packages of a frozen shrimp dish and heated them up. What did I know about cooking? Nothing, but I meant well and made no apologies.

Dear Marty said, "Janice, this is delicious."

Tom and Charley had mutual respect for the other's design talent, but Charley had the last word. Westwood Country Club was his project, and he gave it to Tom. As Tom began sketching, a fellow employee, John Shaw, came to his drawing board and stood silently watching for a moment. A tall, fair-haired fellow, he had a sense of humor as well as a good design sense.

"Beware the boomerang," he said quietly.

Tom looked up at him. "Meaning?"

John smirked. "Meaning a building shape that Charley learned while working for Saarinen."

Sure enough, when Charley made his design rounds, he stood looking at Tom's sketches, which were more in the Bauhaus style of his mentor at Harvard, Walter Gropius.

Tom waited, fearing the boomerang.

Charley took a pen from his white shirt pocket. "How about something a little more dynamic like this?"

A boomerang.

Later Tom and John laughed about it, but Tom designed the best possible boomerang building that wrapped around a swimming pool.

With Arthur's jobs Tom had the freedom to express his ability. Arthur chose Tom to design the Hillview Unit of Brown Schools, a private school for mentally retarded and emotionally disturbed children. When Tom and Arthur went to the site in San Marcos for the first time, they met with both the owner and the headmaster.

"Treat us like your students," Tom said. "Do everything to us like you do when they enter the school."

Westwood Country Club Drawing

12

That was Tom's way of listening and relating to clients. His empathy for the children who would live and learn there was boundless. He became convinced that the school should have a camp-like atmosphere. He divided the project into individual cabins with hipped roofs and wide overhangs. Covered walkways connected the cabins, creating an informal campus that provided a protective environment for children.

The project won a national design award in *Progressive Architecture* magazine's annual competition, both for design and adaptation to the site, which was on a hill overlooking San Marcos. Thus Tom became Arthur's golden boy, as well as an associate in the firm.

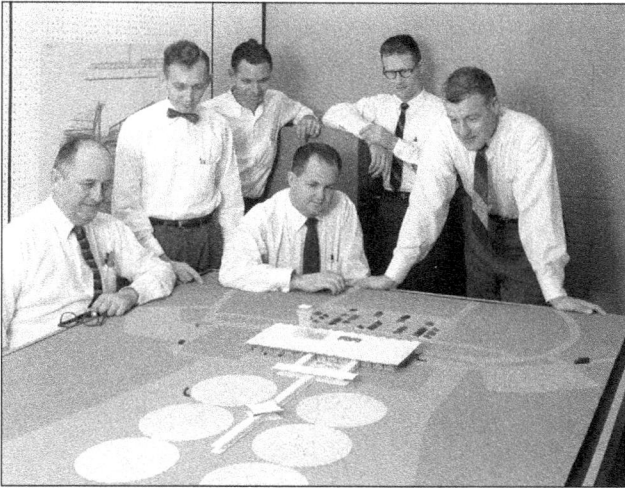

Fehr & Granger Architects

But it was churches rather than schools that became Tom's favorite kind of project to design. It began with the awe he felt as a boy while sitting between his parents in St. Mark's Episcopal Cathedral in Seattle.

He wrote in his memoir, "The gigantic space was designed to look five hundred years old. I sat there entranced with the grandness of the cathedral."

So Tom was delighted when Arthur gave him the job of designing a new sanctuary for Central Presbyterian Church at the corner of Brazos and 8th Street. He loved working with the building committee to achieve the spiritual atmosphere they desired. He was not only a good listener but also had the artistic talent to translate what he heard into inspiring, light-filled spaces. The brilliant stained glass windows are his design as well.

The church was determined to have a grand pipe organ and hired Otto Hoffman, a local organ builder who learned his trade in Germany, to build and install one.

Leaping ahead almost six decades, here are Tom's words from his journal after a visit to the church on November 26, 2016, only a month before he passed away.

> *Just before Thanksgiving I finished my latest watercolor painting. A stunning scene of Central Presbyterian Church interior facing its grand north wall behind the communion table and pulpit. I designed the wall with vertical cedar wood strips. The glorious sound of Otto Hoffman's great organ penetrates the wall between the wood strips. I worked on it as architect with Otto. So sitting in the sanctuary is a memorable visual-audio experience.*

Thus it was fitting and imperative that we have Tom's memorial in that sanctuary which is a crowning glory for him.

Tom's Painting of Central Presbyterian Church

3

I Want a Baby

I took my beloved group of St. Andrew's students through the fourth grade and decided it was time to move on, time to follow my dream of writing for publication. What, I did not know.

While we traveled around the world I wrote about our experiences for the *Asahi Shimbun,* a major Tokyo newspaper that published an English edition. Some of these articles were also published in the *Dallas Morning News.* Tom drew pen and ink illustrations, which added much to the stories and attracted readers' eyes. Even though Tom joked about the fact that I was paid $25.00 for each article and he got only $5.00 for a drawing, we loved working together as writer and illustrator.

But another desire came first because of our friendship with our banker Eddie Wroe and his wife Ammon. One summer night in 1957 they invited us for dinner to see their new baby, their first. When we stepped into the nursery and saw little Eddie peacefully asleep in his bassinet, I yearned to pick him up and cuddle him but did not.

Later at home I told Tom, "I want a baby."

He smiled. "I knew you would change your mind."

"You did?"

"Of course. And your mother wants a grandchild."

I bristled. "That's not the reason."

"What then?"

"Little Eddie awakened my motherly instinct."

"Yes, he's really cute, and big Eddie seems so proud."

"What about you, Tom? Do you want a baby?"

"I could be talked into it," he said with a mischievous grin and a glint in his eyes.

"Well, let's think about it," I said. "It's a life-changing decision."

The next day I left for Dallas to visit my parents for a week. Tom took me to the train station downtown.

"Don't forget to think about it," Tom said, "and I will, too." He embraced me and we said goodbye.

I thought about it all the way to Dallas but said nothing to my parents. When I returned, Tom met me at the train station.

"I've missed you, my queen."

"I've missed you, too, dear Tom."

Back at our apartment, Tom carried in my luggage. "I told them at the office that I wouldn't be back today." He raised his eyebrows and looked at me with big eyes in that suggestive way he always had. "What did you decide?"

"I decided I want you to give me a baby."

"So do I."

Thus was Karl conceived.

For an obstetrician I returned to Dr. Herrod, a fatherly little man who had examined me before marriage.

Pregnancy made me glow and made Tom proud as you can see in this photograph taken at the Texas Society of Architects convention in Dallas in October of 1957. I was two or three months pregnant with Karl who was beginning to show himself. Of course, we did not know who was inside my womb because there was no ultrasound at that time.

TSA Convention 1957

Another photograph from that convention shows us at a costume party. Tom loved dressing up in costumes of his own making. Here he is a clown as in real life, *my* clown who always made me laugh, which is one reason I love him so. In his left hand he holds a miniature violin that he scratched around on during the party, much to everyone's amusement. In his right hand he holds the tail of the fox fur I wore around my neck. I can hardly believe I did so. It was certainly not mine, and I have no idea where it came from.

Costume party

Since we were expecting a baby, Tom and I decided we wanted to move to a better apartment. But where? We were visiting some friends, Lee and Laurel Hodgden, who lived in a one-story apartment complex on Sabine Street, where the LBJ Library now stands. The building had two wings facing each other across a little greenbelt with a ravine. Their apartment had a high-pitched ceiling with exposed beams, very open.

"There's another apartment for rent just like this one across the greenbelt," Laurel told us.

And so we moved there even though it was smaller than our garage apartment. I think we just liked the look and the neighbors. A couple living on the same side but at the other end, Carolyn and Joe Osborn, became good friends of ours, she a writer and he a law student. We have remained friends ever since. In the photo Tom and I are standing on our front porch. I am pregnant and Tom is proud.

Our New Apartment

Now that I was no longer teaching, I decided to enroll in a creative writing course with Professor Gerald Langford, a tall, thin, rather dour man. He gave us assignments and asked authors of the "A" papers to read them aloud for discussion.

"Your first assignment is to recall your earliest memory," he announced, "including the sights and sounds, the smells, all five senses, and how you reacted to them."

I wrote "Daddy's Big Girl," about the time Mother had complications from a miscarriage when I was four years old. I had no idea what was happening, except that she was in the hospital and I feared she might die. I was sent to stay with Aunt Mae and Uncle Grady in Grand Saline.

My story began like this:

> Daddy's hand was big and warm and
> wrapped around mine as we climbed the
> dizzy steps of the train station. I
> looked down at my shiny black shoes.
> Uncle Grady took my other hand in his
> rough one. Together they lifted me high,
> and I flew up, up, up. At the top I
> turned to look down. A shudder went
> through my body, and I held on to Daddy.
> "Is Mother going to die?" I asked him.

Professor Langford gave me an "A." Maybe I *would* grow up to be a writer!

Our new apartment was near the UT campus, so I walked to class three days a week. One day as I passed a construction site, one of the workmen yelled to his fellows.

"Hey, look at what those college boys done."

I was embarrassed but nothing would stop me from continuing to walk to class each day. It never happened again, so perhaps the other guys reprimanded him.

At that time pregnant women did not display their swollen bellies as they do today, which I regret. We draped ourselves in loose clothing as if embarrassed to tell the world that we'd had sex. Even so, maternity clothes spoke for themselves. Mother was an expert seamstress and made all my outfits, even a red taffeta Christmas dress which I loved. In the photo I am sitting on Tom's lap at Mother and Daddy's house. Again, Tom is adoring me.

Pregnant Elegance

We decided on two names: Karl Jordan if the baby was a boy and Anna Tiller if a girl. Karl with a "K" was a name from Daddy's family in Germany, and Jordan was for my maiden name. Anna was a musical name that sounded good with Shefelman, and Tiller was for Mother's maiden name.

Karl arrived later than we anticipated. Dr. Herrod said that was normal for firstborn babies. He was not one to induce labor, and I would not have agreed to it unless medically necessary. Mother came to stay with us on the due date, a week before Karl arrived.

One night I began to have slight labor pains and my water broke. Why do babies so often come during the night? After calling Dr. Herrod, Tom drove the two of us, well three counting baby, to St. David's Hospital, which was nearby. Mother came later.

It was a long labor, again often the case with your firstborn. Mostly I remember the relief between labor pains and dreading their return.

When they did, Dr. Herrod or one of the nurses would say, "Push like you're having a bowel movement." I did. At last a big healthy boy arrived instead, and I cuddled him to my breast. At that time husbands were not allowed in the delivery room, but Karl and I were soon back in my room.

Tom had a big smile on his manly face and his blue eyes shone with love when he saw his eight-plus-pound baby boy.

"He looks a little like Sy Fogel," Tom said, touching Karl's cheek.

"Yes, he does," I said. "Maybe he'll be an artist, too, with you as his teacher and inspiration."

Muscular Dad and Baby Karl

I was intent on nursing Karl even though it was not then the usual choice except, as Dr. Thorne said, with his Latin American mothers! So intent was I that stress decreased my body's ability to make milk, and I had to supplement with formula. Still, it was enough to bond forever. After Karl's birth the cord that connected our bodies was severed. For me, nursing eased that separation.

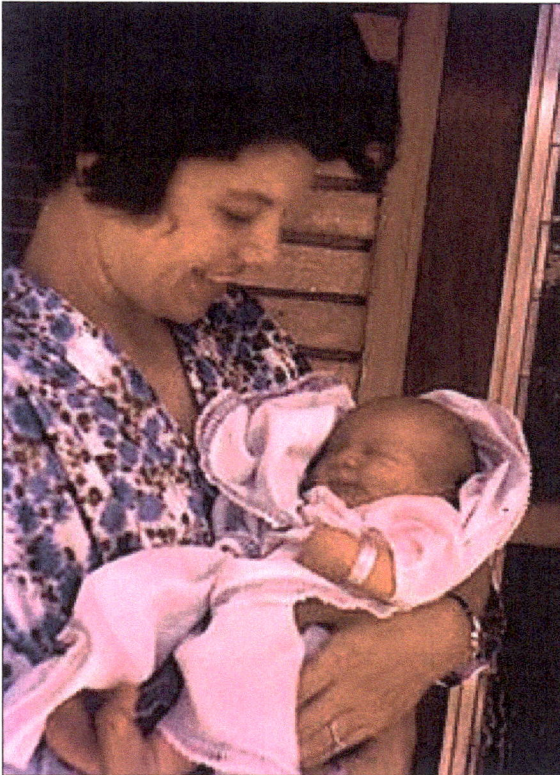

Newborn Karl

After a few days we came home. Mother stayed for a week to help and to enjoy a second motherhood. She lovingly bathed Karl in a baby tub, changed his diapers, and put on the little shirts she had sewn for him. He slept in the same white bassinet where both my brother Terry and I had slept.

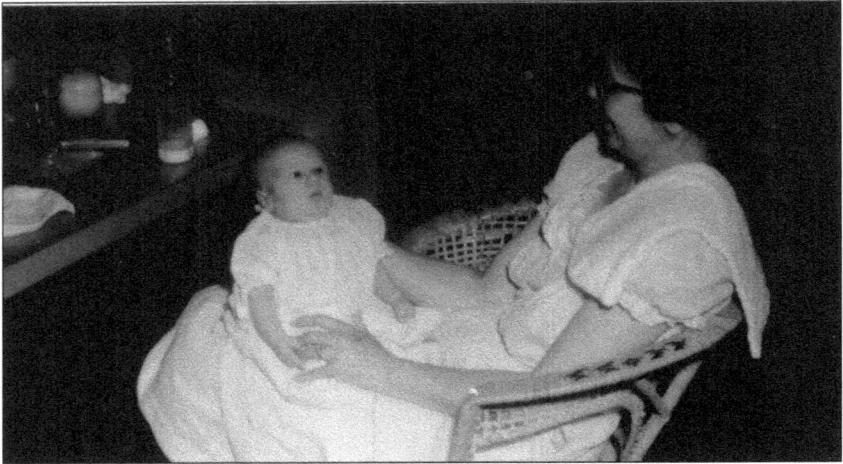

Bebbie with Karl

I, too, loved motherhood and dedicated myself to bringing up my dear little boy. Like most young mothers I had bought a copy of Dr. Spock's *Baby and Child Care*. Thank goodness for this wise pediatrician. I could not have done it without his baby bible. He had ready advice for everything from feeding, burping, and bathing, to changing diapers and potty training. He also encouraged young mothers to follow our maternal instincts. "You know more than you think you do," he wrote.

Every day I took Karl out in the stroller to see the world. Sometimes I walked to Tom's nearby office in the orange brick building. One very cold day I bundled Karl up in his well-insulated blue snowsuit. When I arrived upstairs, Becky and all the architects crowded around to admire him.

"He's our little blue balloon," Herb Crume said.

Yes, this office was a large, loving family.

Soon our little family of three felt the need of a separate bedroom for Karl and an outdoor place where he could play safely. When he was about one year old, we found a duplex on Tom Green Street that had a fenced-in private courtyard. Here Karl stood up and took his first steps.

Once again we were near the UT campus. Tom and I loved central Austin and would never live anywhere else, no matter where we moved.

After dinner we often took a walk, with Tom pushing the stroller. One evening when dusk was falling and the streetlights came on, Karl pointed with his chubby finger.

"Li-i-ight," he pronounced and looked up at me.

I thrilled to his saying this word. "Yes, Karl, light."

It was one of his first words after Mama and Tom. I thought back to a conversation Tom and I had in India when discussing God with a Parsi woman. She said that in her religion they believe God is light. Also, in the *Divine Comedy,* when Dante reaches God, he sees nothing but brilliant, blinding light. Maybe Karl remembered where he came from.

One night before going to bed, I stepped into Karl's room. He was sound asleep, wearing the leg braces he had to have at night to keep his feet from turning outward. It broke my heart to see the braces but they did not seem to bother him. I picked Karl up and put him on my shoulder, then sat in the rocking chair and rocked while singing a made-up lullaby.

> Sleep, baby Karl,
> cause your mama is here,
> keeping your dreams
> from all terror and fear.

It was a tender moment I shall never forget. Does he remember?

Rearranging Bebbie's Pantry

25

Mother was in her glory as a new grandmother, which she yearned to be ever since we returned from our honeymoon. She taught Karl to call her Bebbie, the nickname her younger sister Lillian gave her when trying to say Vera Belle. Daddy, of course wanted to be called Opa, short for the German *Grosspapa*. And so it was.

Karl loved visiting Bebbie and Opa. She took over the mother role when we were there, bathing Karl in the kitchen sink and carefully combing his blond hair. She made clothes for him, shirts, overalls, sunsuits, and she knitted his sweaters. She even let him rearrange her pantry. When Karl was a little older, he also helped Opa rake leaves.

One winter Tom and I decided to return to Aspen where we had met. Karl stayed with his Bebbie and Opa in Dallas while we took the train. Unfortunately, our old lodge was no longer there and Aspen had changed. It had become a place for the rich and fashionable, and we were neither. Even so, we enjoyed the snow and improving our ski technique, except that on one run I panicked and took the chair lift down, which was embarrassing.

When we returned and alighted from the train, Bebbie and Opa were waiting on the platform. Mother held Karl, and when he saw us he hid his face on her shoulder. I still have an image of that heartfelt moment. I took him in my arms and he hugged my neck.

We were all in love with Karl but when he was two years old, our happiness was shattered.

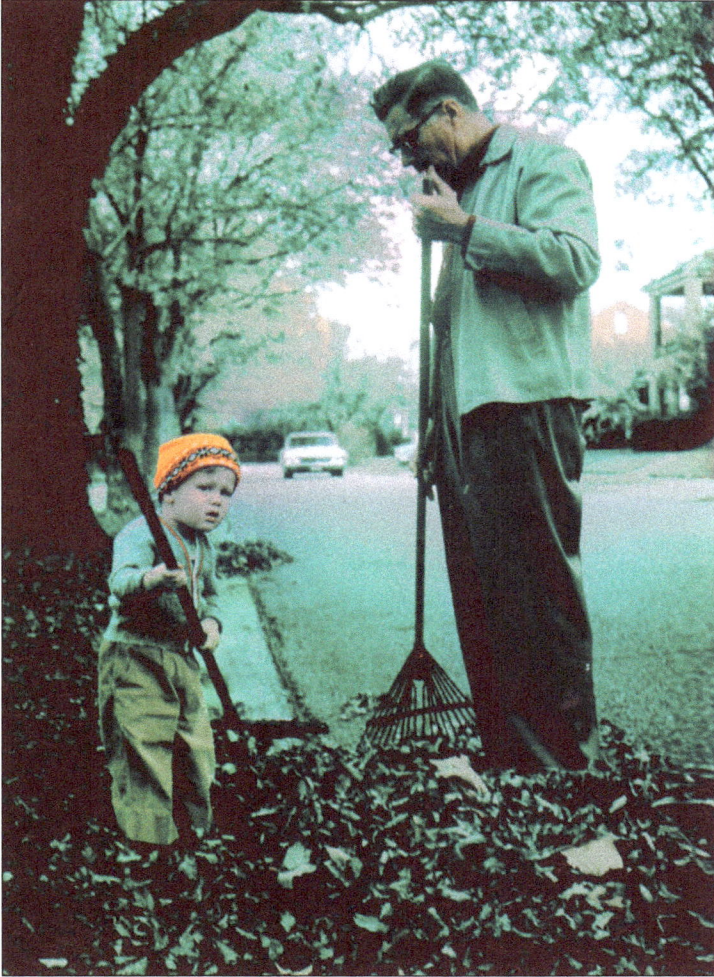

Karl and Opa Rake Leaves

4

A Pall over Our House

I can still see Karl standing at the sliding door, his hands on the glass, his mouth open, crying for us. How could Tom and I walk away? I do not know. Even now the thought gives me a pang of sorrow and regret.

We were headed to the AIA convention in New Orleans where Tom's Harvard professor, Walter Gropius, was a featured speaker. Mother and Daddy were in Europe so I had to hire a babysitter. Karl knew her but she was not me, his mother. Even though Karl soon stopped crying, that was a fateful trip for our family.

In New Orleans Tom enjoyed conversations with Gropius and some of his Harvard Graduate School of Design classmates, but we overindulged in Bourbon Street activity. We drank too much and went to a striptease show. Back at our hotel, we made passionate, abandoned love, and I got pregnant.

Since our family would soon be a foursome, Tom and I thought it was time to stop renting apartments and buy a home. With the help of a realtor we found a Spanish-style house with a red tile roof on Wooldridge Drive overlooking Shoal Creek.

Eddie Joseph, owner of a local theater chain, originally built the house for his young family. Tom would remodel it but not change the vaulted entry on the upper floor with its golden window that looked like the rising sun. The wrought iron gate at the top of the stairway would keep Karl and our prospective baby from falling down into the living room below. Nor would we change that dark-beamed room with its copper-hooded fireplace.

Our First Home

A few months after we moved in, Anna Tiller Shefelman was born. She had multiple congenital problems, probably from my having alcoholic drinks on the night she was conceived. We knew nothing then about the effects of alcohol on a fetus.

Anna had dextrocardia, severe mental retardation, and an extra digit on both hands. We had the latter surgically removed, but nothing could be done about her other problems. Those were the days before ultrasound, so we had no way of knowing about them before she was born. Still, I sensed something was wrong. I did not get very big and she did not move much. I was told that my obstetrician, Dr. McLean, cried when he delivered her.

Mother had come from Dallas to take care of little Karl while I was in the hospital. They had a loving, close relationship, so I had no concerns about him.

Anna stayed in intensive care so I never nursed her or even touched her because parents were not allowed into that room. Thus we never bonded. Just the opposite. I felt ashamed of her, not wanting anyone to see the strange creature we had produced. She had a narrow, pointed forehead and slanted eyes.

After a few days I came home, but she stayed in the hospital for a time. Sweet, blond little Karl lifted my spirits, but there was always the dark despair in my mind. Whether he sensed it I do not know.

Too soon the time came when we had to bring Anna home. She never responded to being held or talked to or kissed. Mother tried to love the poor little creature, bathing her, cuddling her, but there was no use. I just wanted her to die. As Tom told friends, "There is a pall over our house."

We took Anna to Houston to see a neurologist. After examining her, he pronounced her severely retarded. She would never walk or talk or respond. In other words, a vegetable, painful as that sounds. She should have miscarried, and how I wished she had.

I turned most of my attention and all my love to Karl. One time he and I went on a drive with my brother Terry, who was getting his Masters Degree in geography at UT. We stopped at a park somewhere and Karl ran about. Suddenly he tripped and fell on his face but got right up without crying.

Terry said, "Most kids would have come bawling to Mama, but not Karl. He's a tough little kid."

Yes he was and now is a Taekwondo Black Belt, 4th Degree.

Back to Anna. One day I propped her bottle, which I knew was not good, but I felt nothing for her or she for me. I did not even like holding her. Her crib was in our old dining room. In a moment she began to choke on the milk and have one of her seizures during which her body stiffened. I picked her up and patted her back, but she stopped breathing. Quickly I went to Karl's front bedroom where he was building with his blocks.

"Karl, we have to take Anna to the doctor."

He looked at me in surprise. "Why? I'm playing."

"Because she's sick, Karl."

Without another word, he stood and I took him by the hand.

We drove to our pediatrician's office, which was close by. On the way I wondered why I didn't just let her die at home? Fear maybe, fear that I would be blamed. Actually, I think rushing to the doctor was instinctive.

I parked directly in front of the office, picked her up, and ran inside, leaving Karl in the car. *Unbelievable!* A nurse rushed me to the back and took Anna into an examining room. All at once I thought of Karl still in the car and rushed out to the waiting room. There he was, happily playing on a little slide. One of the mothers had run out to get him. As Dr. Price tried to revive her, I sat on a bench outside the examining room and called Tom at his office.

Anna died in the doctor's office, and Tom soon came. We were both shaken, but relieved. When I called my parents, Daddy said, "Thank God." Yes, my thoughts exactly. His words made me feel less guilty for wishing her dead.

Even though Tom and I did not belong to or attend a church, we still thought a clergyman was needed for christenings, weddings, and funerals. Thus Tom asked Reverend Charles Sumners to conduct Anna's funeral service.

Before we married, Tom belonged to St. David's Episcopal Church in downtown Austin, where Charles ministered. He and Tom had disagreements about religious beliefs. Charles seemed convinced that he could change Tom's mind and save his soul.

Once, Tom was explaining how Albert Schweitzer made the point in his *Quest for the Historical Jesus* that Jesus was a man, not a god.

Charles looked at Tom from on high and proclaimed, "He is mistaken, Tom. Jesus was the Son of God, and there is no salvation except through Christ and the church."

Tom said he was not so sure. Still, he stayed with the church until I whisked him away to see the world. Charles may have thought Tom would return to the fold afterward.

It was a mistake to ask Charles to conduct Anna's service. A tall, heavy-set man, he stood facing the audience in his priestly robes, like God himself.

"This is the judgment of God," he said, looking down at us. "Now maybe this young couple will come back to the church."

WHAT? How dare he say that! If only I had stood up and said, *Go to Hell.* But I was too stunned to move or speak. Mother was furious. She never liked Episcopalians anyway.

Days later I called Charles and demanded an apology. He came over to our house. Tom was at work and Charles and I sat on the living room couch, he for once not looking down from on high. We were eye to eye. He apologized, which was satisfying, though I do not remember exactly what he said. I told him we would never set foot in St. David's again, and we never did until after Charles died and went to Hell. Even then it was for a concert, not a service.

Anna was buried at Memorial Hill Cemetery. We never returned to her gravesite until years later and then only because we were at Clark Craig's funeral. She was better forgotten as the pall lifted.

And it soon did with Karl's help. He brought joy back into our home. Sometimes he visited Bebbie and Opa all by himself. Here is a portion of one of the letters Mother wrote to us in 1961:

> *Guess you might like to hear about your son, he is having a wonderful time and says he will go home to Austin in a few days.*
>
> *Right now he is riding his tractor (tricycle) around and around, pulling the little roller rattle toy along behind, says he is Farmer Small planting seed, has on Terry's cowboy hat. You would love to see him.*
>
> *Yesterday when we went to the store. He carried his black purse on his arm just like mine and put on his pipe cleaner glasses and was a scream. He really stopped traffic in the store and did he love the attention. He talks about his Mama and Daddy and says what he thinks you might be doing in Austin.*

Just like his dad, Karl loved drawing and making things. Tom made an easel for him that could hold a big tablet of newsprint paper. It had a shelf for crayons and markers. Karl would stand at this easel and draw, seemingly unaware of anything else. One of his most touching shows the outline of a tall man (Tom) with only one arm that is holding the hand of a little boy (Karl). The other arm was not important.

Tom and Karl Look at Shoal Creek Valley

In 1961 Tom finished the drawings for our house remodeling and work began. In his design the entrance room was turned into a porch like it had originally been. He did the same with the back porch, which had been enclosed. Tom opened up the living room to that porch with a large sliding glass door. But the biggest change was that he knocked out the wall between the old kitchen and dining room and created an open space that became a family room with a new kitchen at the opposite end of the room.

Our contractor friend, Willie, and his father were at our house every day and became almost like family. Sometimes they stopped by the door to Karl's bedroom and watched him drawing at his easel, unaware of his audience. One whole wall of his room was covered with his art.

"Look at that," Willie whispered to me. "He's gonna be an artist or architect just like his daddy."

Tom would often show Karl how to draw people, animals, mountains, trees, trucks, airplanes, anything he was interested in.

One of my great delights as Karl's mama was to read to him. I had a wide knowledge of children's books from a course I took in children's literature at SMU and from years of teaching. Every night before bed, and other times as well, we read while snuggled together on a couch in the family room. Some of his favorites were *Farmer Small, Little Bear, The Biggest Bear, Peter Rabbit*, and especially *Winnie the Pooh*.

Though I am not a devout Christian or even a Christian, I wanted Karl to be like Jesus. I wanted him to love everyone, even his enemies, and turn the other cheek. This was not possible, turning the other cheek, as I discovered when I enrolled him in Polly Sisto's playschool in our neighborhood.

There, Karl first met his longtime friend, Bill Wilson, and for some reason they got into a fight. When I arrived at noon to pick Karl up, the two boys were rolling around on the driveway. Polly and I separated them. Afterward Tom gave Karl wrestling lessons, and never again did he get pinned to the ground. Tom was probably remembering his fight with a bully when he attended junior high school in Tucson, Arizona, and wanted Karl to know how to defend himself. So much for Jesus.

5

And Then Came Daniel

"*I* want a little brother or sister for Karl," I told Tom as we prepared for bed.

Tom came and wrapped his arms around me. "So do I," he said with that suggestive sparkle in his eyes, a look that time cannot take from me. And a look that gave us Daniel.

This time all went well with my pregnancy. I could feel Daniel moving and kicking around. When I started having labor pains one night, my cousin Lin came to our house to stay with Karl, and Tom took me to the hospital. The labor went on and on. Daniel wanted out of there but he had tilted his head back and could not get out. To save us both, a Caesarian birth was the only choice. Dr. McLean cut my belly open and lifted Daniel out. For all that struggle, he was a big healthy boy, another eight pounder. What a relief!

"I'm delighted with him," the pediatrician, Dr. Wilborn, said.

So were Tom and I and our families. Without the tragedy of Anna, we would not have Daniel, a blessing out of a curse.

Mother soon arrived and took charge of everything at our home. She was shocked that I had to have a Caesarian birth, but I was happy that Daniel got out okay. Karl had just turned four, and Tom brought him to the garden at St. David's Hospital where I could wave to him from the hospital window. I was more relaxed nursing Daniel, but supplemented with formula later. I can remember how he liked to finger the mole on my neck as I held him in my arms.

We named him Daniel Whitehead Shefelman. Daniel was a name from Opa's family that went back to Germany. Whitehead was Tom's middle name and his mother's maiden name.

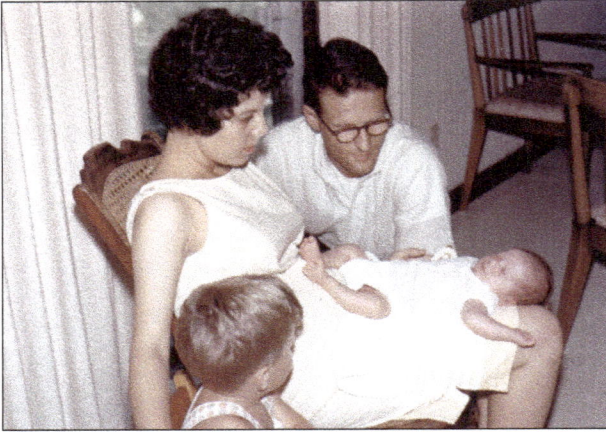

Our Baby Daniel

For four years Karl had us to himself. On his birthday he got a puppy, Beagie, and soon after, a little brother. Karl took to Daniel better than to Beagie who made loud, sharp barks and sad, high-pitched howls. Karl never liked loud noises. Beagie roamed the neighborhood and one day he didn't come back.

When the time came that Tom and I needed our private bedroom and Daniel needed his, we moved downstairs. Karl took our bedroom with the tall arched window overlooking Shoal Creek and Daniel took Karl's. So big brother got the bedroom with a view.

As Daniel said from the pulpit at Tom's memorial, following Karl's eulogy:

"... the thing about being the little brother is that the big brother gets to do everything first and so used up all my ideas." Then flipping open a page of the Bible, he said, jokingly, "So I'm just going to read out of the Bible." Audience laughter.

Still, the advantage to being the younger brother is that by then Tom and I had learned how to be Mother and Father Bear. With a husband and two sons, I felt like the queen of the household. Perhaps it was true because later Tom began to call me his queen.

Karl did not seem to resent sharing us with Daniel. Just the opposite. He was protective, perhaps because he was definitely the big brother by four years. One time at Opa's ranch when Daniel was probably one year old, we put him up on a tree branch beside Karl, who was a devoted tree climber. He held on to Daniel with both arms.

Boys in a Tree

At home Karl and Daniel would sit on the couch with a book while Karl read/told him the story and they talked about the illustrations.

They both loved staying at Bebbie and Opa's house in Dallas while Tom and I had a little vacation. Karl wrote this letter to us.

> DEAR JANICE AND TOM
> DANIEL AND I TOOK A BATH IN THE SINK.
> I HAVE RIDED MY TRICYCLE EVERY DAY.
> DANIEL IS A GOOD BOY.
> I AM GOING TO HOLLANDS TODAY.
> I LOVE YOU
>
> KARL

On a later visit as Bebbie was hugging Daniel goodnight, he said, "I love you, Bebbie, but I love Mama more." Sweet.

Daniel did have me to himself when Karl spent the mornings at Polly Sisto's playschool. She was a loving, masterful teacher who knew how to encourage young children to play and work together, even though there was an occasional little fight, as with Karl and Bill. But Polly, as well as Tom, made that a learning experience.

There were tricycles and small cars galore and a long driveway where the children could ride. Also a sandbox, swing set, and a jungle gym.

At that time Juanita Swisher, a black woman, worked for us, cleaning our house and watching over the boys when I went out. We all loved her and every Christmas took a turkey to her family who lived on the east side. One morning I asked Juanita to drive Karl to playschool.

Little fair-haired Karl looked up at me with a worried expression on his face. "Will they think Juanita is my mother?"

Juanita and I laughed, and she assured Karl that they would not.

Karl wrote: "I ate play-doh on a regular basis, made the usual toilet paper tube art projects, played in the sandbox and on the jungle gym with the rest of the kids. One time, after holding it too long on the playground, I peed on the assistant teacher's dress the second she yanked my pants down before she could get me in front of the toilet. I had to wait in the bathroom for my mother to come with dry pants."

When I brought his pants, the kind older lady smiled and said, "This isn't the first time I've been peed on!"

Karl also remembers this story. "One time my mom came running into the playground to pick me up, announcing one of my little classmates had just been hit by a car in front of the school. He recovered, but I remember him returning to school days later with dark bruises all over. His name was Ronnie and to this day I associate that name with a bruised young boy."

In spite of what I said when Tom proposed, I took to bringing up boys and nourishing their minds and bodies. It became my purpose in life. I wanted Karl and Daniel to have a perfect childhood and did my best to give them one. Maybe I should have given more thought to their becoming adults. But I think I did the right thing so that they could retain the child inside and become creative artists. Anyway, I love what they have become — sensitive, creative, strong, gentle men. Of course, they had a perfect model in Tom.

Both boys called their father Tom. I think that was because when I spoke to them about Tom I used his name instead of Daddy for fear Tom and I would start calling each other Mama and Daddy like some other couples.

I taught Karl and Daniel to call me Mama, in remembrance of my beloved east Texas grandmother. As they got older, Mama became Mom. So it was Mom and Tom. Later Karl felt uncomfortable referring to his father as Tom and began calling him Dad. As Karl said at Tom's memorial service, "It feels natural now."

Even though I did not like to cook, I learned because I wanted our family to enjoy tasty, wholesome food together. We always gathered for breakfast, dinner, and sometimes lunch. The Shefelmen's praise and some of Mother's recipes soon made a good cook out of me. They especially loved French toast on Wednesday mornings, waffles on Sunday, and dinners like butterfly fried shrimp and ground beef stroganoff.

I became interested in health foods such as whole grains and organic produce. Karl recently reminded me that sometimes we had ice cream with wheat germ sprinkled on top. The boys didn't know any better. I even learned how to bake whole wheat bread. There were no Cokes or Dr. Peppers in our refrigerator, but I did serve them treats like homemade oatmeal chocolate chip cookies and Daniel's beloved mint chocolate chip ice cream from Bluebell.

Chocolate was a favorite for all of us. For our birthdays I made a dark chocolate cake with chocolate icing adapted from Helen Corbett's cookbook. Later it became known as "The Cake." Daniel learned to make it for his children, Lena and Will, even mailing a frozen cake to Lena when she was at Kenyon College.

He had taken an early liking to cooking when I bought *Betty Crocker's Cookbook for Boys and Girls*. One of the recipes was polka dot macaroni. It became a family favorite — not the wholesomest food with Velveeta cheese and sliced wieners for dots, but easy to prepare and fun to look at. From there Daniel went on to making Bebbie's banana cupcakes and now cooks for his own family and sometimes me when he visits.

Chef Daniel

I read the same books to Daniel that I read to Karl but also some new ones. We gave Daniel another Little Bear story for Christmas called *Father Bear Comes Home*, which I loved as much as he did. The Mother, Father, Little Bear relationship is so tender. Their closeness almost made me cry. I wanted to be like Mother Bear.

Daniel's all-time favorite was *Choo Choo* by Virginia Lee Burton. Every night, it seemed, he asked for *Choo Choo*. Maybe because it's about a shiny black engine that runs away from its train. And because of the lively black and white and red illustrations.

Both Karl and Daniel loved *Goodnight Moon*. The text is rhythmic and lulling, the illustrations cozy. What a comforting great green bedroom with mother rabbit sitting and knitting in a rocking chair. The ending, "Goodnight noises everywhere," brings the whole world together in peace. My boys always played the game of finding the mouse in each illustration.

Even when they learned to read, I kept on reading to them. *D'Aulaires'*
Book of Greek Myths was a great favorite and influence in their lives.

Reading Greek Myths

In the sixth grade Karl excelled in a report on Greek gods. Daniel
instilled this love of Greek myths in his own children, prompting Will
to major in classics at Johns Hopkins. Knowledge of these myths led
to reading versions of Homer's *Iliad* and *Odyssey*. We also read all the
Little House books, *Johnny Tremain,* and the seven *Chronicles of Narnia,*
to name a few.

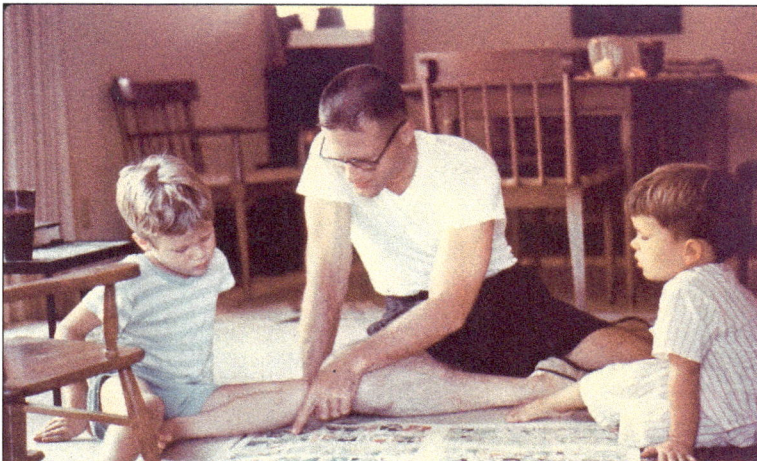

Reading the Sunday Comics

Appropriately, Tom read the Sunday funnies to them. To quote Karl, "Dad had his own unique ways of showing his love and affection for us. He would sit on the family room floor with us and read the entire Sunday funny papers, complete with funny cartoon voices."

Tom and I each developed our own goodnight routines, though Tom's was not very conducive of sleep. In Karl's words: "I fondly remember his ritual of coming in our rooms to say good night, sitting on our bed, and bopping us in the head and face with Winnie the Pooh and the variety of other stuffed animals we slept with, again making funny sounds and voices of each character. This went on well into sixth grade, by the way, until it was leaked out at school that I still slept with Winnie the Pooh, at which point it all stopped and the animals were put away in a basket."

Goodnight Tom Style

My routine was gentler. I sat on their beds and we talked about events of the day or about concerns either of them might have. And then it was, "Nighty-night and sweet dreams," followed by a butterfly kiss with my eyelashes on their cheeks.

Once, when Karl was eight years old, he said, "Mama, I'm having mortality thoughts."

"About who?"

"About you and Tom."

My throat tightened and I cupped his cheeks in my hands. "Karl, Tom and I will be here for a very long time. Don't you worry." I leaned close and gave him a butterfly kiss. "Now nighty-night and sweet dreams."

Karl always responded with, "Nighty-night. Have a nice little party and have fun."

I'm not sure how that response started but it endured. Maybe it began one night when we were entertaining downstairs.

Daniel had concerns too but voiced them in a different way. We had a speaker installed in the hall between the boys' bedrooms so that we could hear them from our downstairs bedroom. I would hear Daniel begin to whimper, "Nnnnhhh, nnnnhhhh." And then he would be kneeling at our bedside, his head next to me, sucking his thumb. He never told me why he was worried, and eventually I would take him back upstairs and all was well.

Dr. Thorne called the problem "night terrors," or childhood nightmares. Later, Karl began sleepwalking and once ended up in Daniel's bed. I was concerned, but Dr. Thorne said it was common with the hormonal changes of becoming an adolescent.

Like Karl, Daniel began drawing very early with Tom's encouragement and instruction. One of my favorites is a drawing he did of Tom and me, probably at age three. Our heads are large ovals with smiles on our faces. Tom's eyes are small dots close together and his nose a long straight line. He has a crewcut. My eyes are circles and my hair is scribbly with curls. These faces have no bodies, just stick legs, with Tom leaning toward me. Daniel got us and our feelings exactly.

When Karl turned five, I enrolled him in a private kindergarten, since at that time it was not offered in public school. Jeanette Watson's school came highly recommended. Indeed, years later, the governor appointed her Director of the Texas Office of Early Childhood Development, where she pushed for reform. Jeanette was a small dark-haired woman of infinite patience and knowledge about how to treat five-year-old children and help them grow. Karl adored her.

Daniel at the Easel

The kindergarten was in the lower floor of her home and opened onto a big garden where the children played. Karl wore clothes that Bebbie made for him until Jeanette suggested I might dress him in jeans like the other boys, which I did. Perhaps they had made fun of his corduroy overalls. Karl never complained, but I trusted her judgment.

One day Jeanette and some parents, including Tom and me, took the whole group on a train ride to San Marcos. At a playground there were monkey bars. Tom jumped up, grabbed a bar, and hanging by his arms, walked with his hands to the other end. Then Karl held up his arms, Tom lifted him so he could grab a bar, and together they hand walked, Tom right behind Karl. Jeanette was charmed by their father-son relationship.

When Daniel was three years old, our neighbor, Nancy Newman, and I decided to start a playday for her John and my Daniel.

"I know two other friends who have three year olds and might like to join us, Camille Shannon and Carole Sikes," she said.

And so it was. Once a week we met at one another's homes for Daniel, John, Little Camille, and Laura Sikes to play. Our favorite place was Camille's. The Shannons had a two-story colonial house on a large property on Windsor Road. There was even a basketball court. Sometimes we moms and our children, including Karl during the summer months and Camille's older sister, played basketball together. Big Camille, who delighted in calling Daniel "Danielle," was a beautiful and gracious redheaded lady, but on the basketball court she became fiercely competitive. Unbelievable! After a time the little ones would wander away to play and leave us to our game.

The Sikes lived near us on Churchill Drive in a house designed by Tom's fellow Gropius student, Chester Nagle. The house had a limestone wall facing the street, big windows opening up on both sides and a balcony overlooking Shoal Creek in the back.

Years later when the Sikes sold the house, Tom was asked to do some remodeling for the new owners. Naturally he respected the existing design, so the added stairwell and updated kitchen look as if they were part of the original house.

One day we moms were sitting in the back garden talking as the children played when Daniel screamed and came running to me holding out his little hand, which had red dents.

"Laura bit me!" he said with tears in his eyes.

I took his hand in mine and looked. There was no blood, just teeth marks.

"Oh, Daniel, does it hurt?"

"Ye-e-s-s-s," he cried.

"Here, let me kiss it." I took him in my lap and comforted him.

Meanwhile, Carole Sikes brought Laura to us, took her hand and bit it. Laura let out a yell.

"Now you know how that feels," Carole said. "Tell Daniel you're sorry."

Laura hid her face on her mother's front and mumbled, "I'm sorry."

It was enough and never happened again, and Daniel graduated to Polly Sisto's playschool the next year and then to Jeanette Watson's kindergarten. We had a kindergarten carpool for Daniel, John Newman, second cousin Marc Shivers, and Christine Coffee, daughter of an architect friend. Blond, curly-haired Christine was the carpool princess. I think all three boys were in love with her.

Daniel was a favorite of Jeanette's but perhaps she made each child feel like a favorite. That was her charm and her ability.

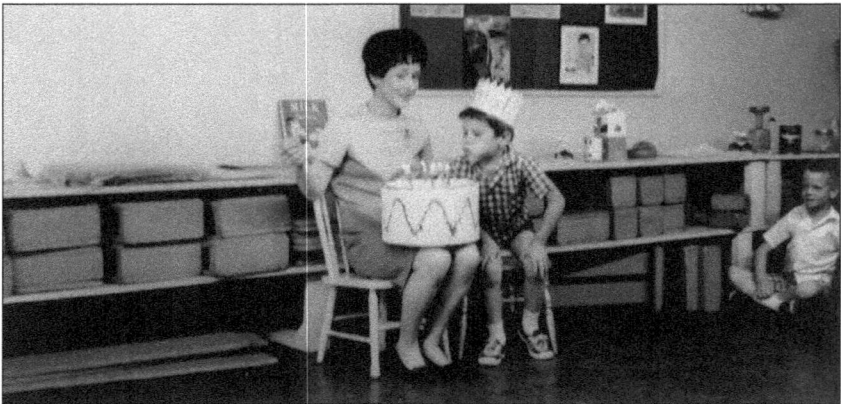

Daniel's Chosen Birthday

She also made all the children with all their differences feel an important part of the group. She treated behavior problems with kindness. Those children who had a birthday during the summer got to celebrate a "Chosen Birthday," complete with a crown and muffins supplied by moms. For Daniel it was Bebbie's banana muffins, which he, as king for a day, proudly handed out to each child.

As the boys got older, Karl sometimes bullied Daniel. Once when he shoved Daniel and made him cry, Tom became angry, put Karl over his knees, and spanked him.

I remember comforting Daniel while calling out, "No, Tom, stop."

Karl and Daniel were both crying and so was I. That was the only time Tom ever spanked either of our boys.

6

Home and Neighborhood

*A*bout home, Daniel said in his eulogy for Tom: "There's a quote in an amazing book called *The Poetics of Space* that says: 'The house shelters daydreaming. The house protects the dreamer. The house allows one to dream in peace.'

"And that's how Tom's houses were that he built for us. He remodeled the first house and designed and built the second one around us. He made sure that we had a safe house. The influence of the space you grow up in is the strongest psychological and emotional influence you'll ever have. Even if you don't still live in that house, you will always be defined by it."

Our home on Wooldridge Drive was in Pemberton, an upscale, tree-lined neighborhood where children could freely roam on foot or bicycle. We overlooked Shoal Creek and the new Hike and Bike Trail, an area that Karl, Daniel, and their friends called "downbelowthecliff." Our access to the trail was across Bill Carter's and Mrs. Fridell's backyards to Mrs. Wild's where a part of the cliff had broken away, making a walkable but not rideable slope. Below was a pond where Shoal Creek had been dammed for the trail to cross, and a giant split rock rose above it. Thus the area was called Split Rock. The children could play as if in the wild, and I could call them home with an old school bell.

The trail along Shoal Creek was a favorite outing for the boys and me, and on weekends Tom joined us. There is a great old live oak almost to Pease Park that we named the Climbing Tree, and that's just what Karl and Daniel did. It has enormous low, almost horizontal branches, making it easier to climb. There was something spiritual about that tree, holding our sons on its rough branches. It seemed protective and loving.

Climbing Tree

Karl's best friend, Bill Wilson, lived only three houses away, also overlooking Shoal Creek. When Karl and Bill were only five years old, playing at Bill's house, they decided to ride their tricycles along Wooldridge Drive to Claire Avenue, then down the hill to the Hike and Bike Trail, unbeknownst to Betty Wilson.

Mrs. Wild was driving home in her Cadillac and saw them riding down the side of the street toward the creek. She stopped at our house to tell me. I jumped in her car, we picked up Betty, and drove down there. Sure enough, Karl and Bill had started riding on the Hike and Bike Trail.

I was so relieved to see them safe that I just ran and hugged Karl.

Betty stood with her hands on her hips. "Bill, don't ever do this again without telling me."

I realized I needed to be a disciplinarian too, and said, "Yes, Karl, you gave us quite a scare."

When we were back home, I told Karl, "We'll just wait and see what Tom says about this."

Although I could tell that Karl was worried about what would happen, Tom did not scold or punish him. Instead he said, "I'm disappointed in you, Karl." That was Tom's method of discipline, and it worked. Karl never did it again. We now refer to this little adventure as "The Tricycle Trip."

I loved walking in the neighborhood with Karl and Daniel, first with tricycle and stroller and later trike and bike. We walked along Wooldridge Drive, up to Hardouin to Harris Boulevard and back along Wooldridge. We knew every house, yard, tree, and flower along the way by memory. We had our stopping places to climb a tree or smell the flowers.

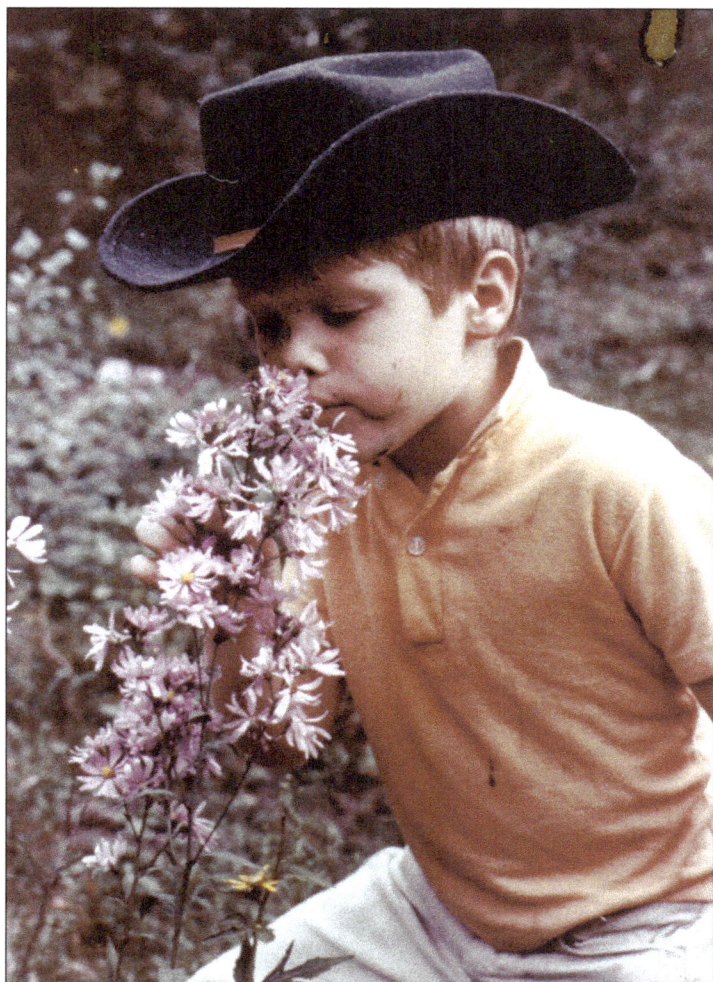

Smelling the Flowers

Karl always loved to smell flowers wherever he found them. Today he takes pride in the morning glories he raises on his Manhattan balcony. Daniel grows flowers in his garden, including sunflowers. That love makes me happy because real men love flowers.

One scary incident happened on this walk that is seared in my memory. As I pushed baby Daniel in the stroller, Karl rode ahead on his tricycle, both of us safely on a sidewalk set back from Wooldridge Drive and a distance from the mansions that line the street. We came to a downward slope where Karl loved to lift his feet and let his tricycle coast. Suddenly a car came backing out of a long driveway — fast, headed for Karl.

"STOP, KARL," I screamed.

He threw himself and his tricycle onto the grass, stopping just in time. The driver never noticed and proceeded down the street. From then on Karl and I both looked for cars backing out.

A place where Karl and Daniel always wanted to get off their vehicles and sit for a moment was at some steps that led up to the front yard of a white stucco cottage. Bushes sheltered the steps, and the boys liked sitting there. Little did we know that clients of Tom's would buy that house one day and Tom would renovate it into a Tudor mini-mansion, complete with half timbers and an English front garden.

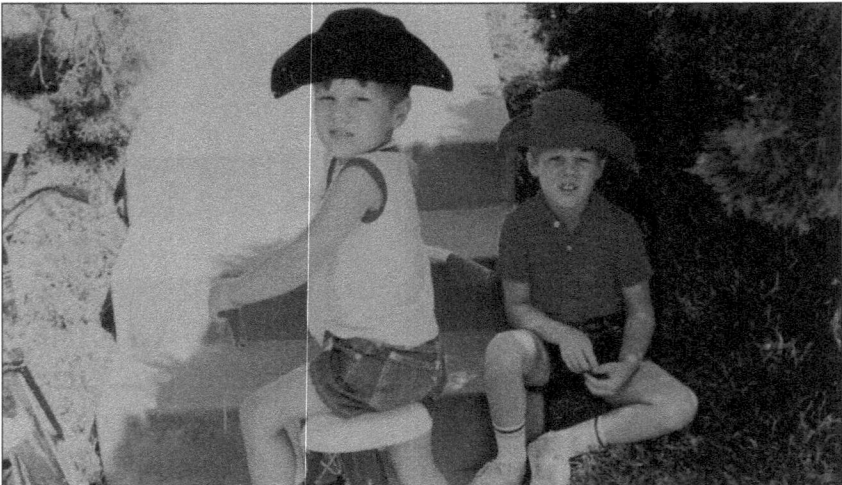

Trike and Bike Walk

Another walk we used to take was in the neighborhood of the washateria I used. Since I had no washer and dryer at home, I packed up our laundry in two baskets and, with the boys in tow, drove over to the washateria on 24th Street, across from the then Kash-Karry grocery store. After putting the laundry in the washers, I unloaded Karl's tricycle and Daniel's stroller and off we went into the residential neighborhood near the UT campus.

Our neighborhood gained another play activity when the Wilsons built a swimming pool overlooking Shoal Creek. Karl and Daniel enjoyed it so much that sometimes Jim Wilson had a problem getting Daniel out of it.

"Daniel, get out of the damn pool!"

Not to be intimidated, Daniel took his time. I don't know how Jim put up with it but he did.

Some years later Tom and I decided to build a pool, filling in the lower level of our backyard. During the winter of 1973-74 construction began. To our horror, the owner of the company was riding in a Bobcat to level the ground, and the scraper caught under the railing and flipped him over the 30-foot cliff, Bobcat and all. Daniel was watching from the back porch and started yelling. After I called 911, we climbed down and saw that the man had landed on the roof of the Bobcat, still belted in.

The emergency crew brought a stretcher, lifted him out, and whisked him away to the hospital, where he recovered. For a time I worried that Daniel was traumatized. We talked it over and over, and I reassured him that it was not our fault and that the man was okay.

I never thought of myself as the type to have a private swimming pool. It just seemed like a good thing to do for the boys. Daniel and the neighborhood kids enjoyed our pool but Karl, being a teenager by then, preferred going to a public pool where more friends and girls hung out.

Daniel's best friend, John Newman, lived around the corner from our house, as did Reed Stephenson and Stuart Schwiff. Reed's older sister, red-headed Cottie, enjoyed playing with the neighborhood boys, and they were all in love with her. Both Karl and Daniel had childhood girlfriends. Karl says his first girlfriend was either Julie Shapiro, whom he met at Polly Sisto's playschool, or Simone Joseph, the blonde granddaughter of Harry and Helen Joseph across the street. Whenever she visited, Mrs. Joseph invited Karl over to play. Daniel's first was either Barbara Day who lived two doors down the street or Leah Fisher, also blonde, from Polly Sisto's playschool.

Daniel and John

The neighborhood children invented their play, their make-believe characters and disguises as cowboys, soldiers, Achilles, Thor, firemen, whatever they fancied themselves to be. They made their own rules and even their own movies.

Karl and Bill made construction paper mustaches, epaulettes, badges, and military rank stripes. Bill had an old-timey pistol tucked in his belt, and Karl carried a rifle. Together they kept law and order.

I had not believed in letting Karl and Daniel have play guns. But they had their way, using sticks for guns, so I gave in. Eventually they had a BB gun, and Daniel accidentally shot our neighbor's window and broke it. David Edwards was furious.

"Why do you allow your sons to play with guns?"

I shook my head and apologized. In my defense though, I have to say that he had no sons.

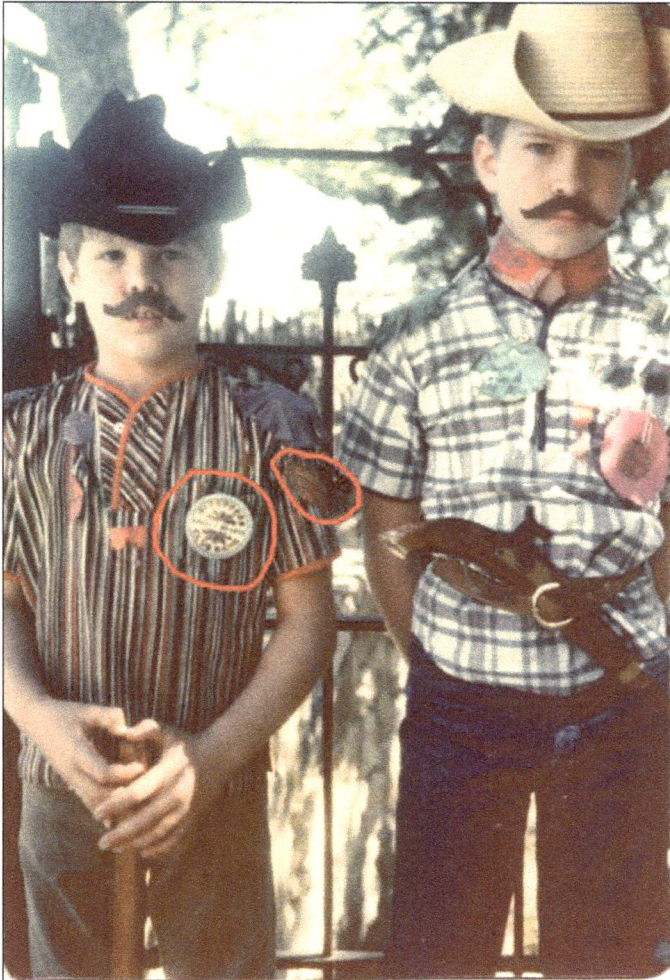

Karl and Bill Play Soldiers

"They're so serious," said one of our older neighbors who never married or had children.

Yes, for children play can be serious since it is creating a reality and practicing life, come what may. I believe this play made them the creative men they are.

Both boys created worlds in their rooms with wooden blocks, Lincoln Logs, Tinkertoys, and Lego. They made buildings, towers, towns, farms, cabins, and forts. They played with miniature cowboys, Indians, animals, and soldiers, all the while becoming those characters.

They each had a whole wall covered in burlap that served as a place to display their drawings. And each had a big desk made by Tom where they built model airplanes and ships, drew, and did homework. Daniel's room had a round particleboard table, also made by Tom, and two child-size chairs. On Thursday nights Karl and Daniel had dinner there and watched *Daniel Boone* on our small black-and-white TV.

Daniel and Blocks

At Daniel's request we bought a Super 8 movie camera, which both boys used. They made movies with neighborhood kids, one of which was a stop-action film of scooting around on their bottoms as if in a car. This camera was the beginning of film careers for both boys. Daniel moved on to making an animated film called *Dink*. It is about two egg friends. Dink saves Donk from being eradicated by an eraser. Daniel submitted the film to the statewide Fifth Annual Student Film Festival and won favorite of the festival.

Karl and Bill Admire Their Tower

Snow at Our House

Sledding in Shoal Creek Valley

Occasionally Austin had snow, yes snow, sometimes almost a foot deep! We even had a sled, and Tom and I would take the boys down-belowthecliff, via 29th Street and slide around. As they got older, the neighborhood children gathered at the top of Gaston Avenue and slid down the hill to the creek on pasteboard boxes.

While children on the other side of Wooldridge Drive and beyond were assigned to Bryker Woods Elementary, we were assigned to Wooldridge Elementary, which was across Lamar on 24th Street, near the UT campus. After visiting the latter, Tom and I decided to send Karl to Dill Elementary where the Wilsons were sending Bill. It was an open school with first through third grades only, perfect for a very young child. From there they moved on to Casis Elementary. Both were experimental schools connected with the U.T. education department.

Naturally Tom and I wanted the best education available for Karl and Daniel, but more than academic success, we yearned for our boys to keep and develop their creative powers. We believed in being involved in their schools. I was president of Dill Elementary School PTA when Daniel was a student there.

Teachers encouraged parents to visit school and we did.

Karl remembers the time in Mrs. Anderson's third grade when Tom visited his class and showed the children the process of making blueprints. He brought blueprint paper for each child and they went out into the grassy courtyard. The children gathered leaves, twigs, rocks, anything they wanted to put on the paper, some even putting their hands on it for a brief exposure to the ultra violet rays of the sun. Then they returned to the classroom and Tom inserted their papers, one by one, into the blueprint machine he had brought. The ammonia in the machine turned their papers blue with white images.

Daniel remembers the time Tom came to his fifth grade class at Casis to talk about drawing. In his eulogy for Tom he said:

"He drew these insanely complicated contour drawings of human figures and perspectives. I looked around the class and they were sort of like … blank. It meant nothing to them. They had no idea what he was talking about. I was so mortified, but now I'm proud."

My favorite school involvement was volunteering in the Casis library where Helen Keel was librarian. Really, I think she and Alice McGuire, who established the library in the beginning, were the inspiration that led me to later become a librarian at Lake Travis Elementary. At Casis I did every kind of job from shelving books, repairing books according to Helen's instruction, to storytelling for first-grade classes in the library. This job fit with an emerging purpose in my life, writing children's books.

It was a library book that inspired Daniel to organize the John Muir Nature Club when he was ten years old after reading a biography of the man. They published a newsletter and planned a hike up Shoal Creek to find the source.

One early morning in the summer, Daniel set out with John, Reed, and school friends, Peter Larkam and Steven Anderson, whom Daniel admired for his early muscular development and attractiveness to girls. Each had a backpack with snacks and water.

It is hard to believe that the other mothers and I allowed them to go alone. I worried the whole time and drove upstream to watch for them at one of the bridges. As I waited I saw them trudging along the trail and they seemed okay. I resisted the urge to call out to them because I wanted Daniel to have an adventure; and they did, surviving mud, dogs, an angry resident, and a friendly one. And most amazing, the boys succeeded in finding the spring on the grounds of the Balcones Research Center, some eight miles to the north, and returned home, hungry and tired.

By this time we had a new neighbor. Back when we first bought our house, we could not afford to buy the lot next door, even though it was part of the original Joseph property. We did have an option to buy the lot if anyone made an offer. Our old sailing friend, Bill Carter, made an offer and we opted out. I always regretted that decision because several great old live oaks grew there. But we had no choice financially.

To Tom's disappointment, Bill hired another sailor friend, Eugene George, to design his home. Maybe Bill worried that Tom had too much at stake, living next door. Bill was a good neighbor but his house was not. It didn't fit in with other houses on the street. Neither did Bill, who grew marijuana in his backyard. He did fit in with Karl and Daniel and friends because he had a workshop downstairs where he made gliders and helped the neighborhood boys make theirs with his materials and advice. Then they flew the gliders in his backyard. Sometimes one went over the cliff and had to be retrieved by the boys.

But the best workshop of all for Karl and Daniel was Tom's. It was a real man cave where they made stuff. To quote Karl from his eulogy for Tom:

"Many fathers and sons bond by watching and enjoying sports, the world of men. Instead, my father bonded with us through drawing, building and creating. Countless hours were spent in the workshop, which was attached to the garage where he had his tool bench, vice, and every tool imaginable, and my brother and I had our smaller child-size version. We made all sorts of things, wire coil magnets, crude furniture, tree houses, even a go-cart made from the aluminum frame of an old lawn chair we found in the garbage, complete with a real steering wheel and canvas seat."

As for tree houses, there were three. First a triangular open platform designed by Tom and attached to one of the catalpa trees in our backyard. Then came a two-level box house that Tom and Daniel built together. And finally a cliffhanger built by Tom and Karl.

Tom and the boys also bonded with drawing. They drew each other, they drew themselves, they drew me. I'm the only one who did not draw. I ran our home, nourished them, read to them, read to myself, and worked at writing for children.

Tom gave them lessons in figure drawing, although Daniel's figures often turned into monsters and still do. He taught them perspective drawing as well. Both boys revere their father's ability to draw and his intuitive mastery of perspective.

Daniel's Tree House

As Karl said at Tom's memorial:

"Dad is my first and best art teacher. He taught me how to truly see the world as an artist, and I will carry his wisdom and talent forward in my own art, heart, and mind as long as I live." Sob.

And Daniel said:

"I teach illustration and animation and I talked to my students when my father was very sick. I told them ninety percent of what I tell you came from him. So pay attention.

"He taught me about negative space, which in the act of drawing is very important. It's everything that isn't the drawing.

"I remember we had figure drawing class. People always ask me, where did you go to art school? I didn't go to art school. My dad taught me everything. And I had some art school afterward but the structure of everything I know was from him. How to make a little skeleton under your character. I'm still teaching that."

Not only did Tom and I hope the boys would follow artistic careers, we wanted them to be citizens of the world, not just of Texas or America, so we put up a wall map of the world in our family room beside the dining table. I think we succeeded, in that both Karl and Daniel went away to college in Ohio and eventually moved to New York to pursue their careers. In Daniel's case, also to pursue Jane. And fortunately, there Karl found Ellen. Though I wish they lived closer, it is partly my fault.

We also wanted Karl and Daniel to grow up with pets. After Beagie ran away, we decided on dachshunds, first Schotzie and later Theo. Both seemed to have an inferiority complex. Both chased cars, barking all the way. Schotzie, who slept at the foot of either Karl's or Daniel's bed, would growl at anyone who came in.

Tragically, Schotzie savagely killed the Newman's newborn kittens. Nevertheless we remained friends and are even closer friends today since John lives in New York and Nancy lives here in Westminster. Schotzie was later killed while chasing a car. Then Theo survived a fall over the cliff but eventually got in a fight with the Days' Weimaraner and lost.

Karl's Tree House

Finally we decided on a border collie, Max, who was stolen. Our best and last dog, another border collie, this one a female who Tom named Bonnie. She turned out to be the sweetest, smartest dog ever.

Karl, Daniel, and I took her to a breeder, and the minute she went into the fenced yard a male mounted her right in front of us. He did not waste a minute. Sure enough she gave birth to a litter of puppies in our family room as the boys and I watched. One of the puppies could not get out of the birth sac.

"Mama, do something," Karl wailed.

I thought Bonnie would instinctively know what to do because I did not. If only I had broken the sac, the puppy would have survived but he suffocated before I figured it out, and we buried him in the side yard. We still had six wiggling, squirming, suckling puppies, gave one to Aunt Mae, and sold the others.

We also had several cats, one after another as they wandered in. Puffin had kittens under Daniel's watchful eyes. We gave them away and had no more.

Bonnie is the pet we all remember most tenderly. Since she was a sheep and goat herder, she was in her glory at Opa's ranch, going on hikes with us, herding us and sometimes goats.

Bonnie

7

Meanwhile Back at the Ranch

Daddy, or Opa as the boys called him, inherited 1600 acres of land from his father, Daniel Jordan. He gave all his children land that he had acquired over the years, but since Daddy was the only one who chose to be an academic instead of a rancher or a rancher's wife, he did not get prime land. Instead he got land in the hills west of Mason and named it Blue Mountain Ranch, better for goats than cattle. Dramatic land with hazy mountains, springs, and creeks.

In the beginning Daddy had the Ellebracht family living there in a small primitive house, raising goats on the rocky hills. His family and Daddy's were old acquaintances in Mason.

As a child I loved visiting the ranch with Daddy and watching the goats being sheared in the spring. Chester Ellebracht was my age and we enjoyed playing together. There were two other children, James and Ruthie.

Their mother, Annie, was a sturdy woman who cooked meals on a wood stove. We, along with Dan, the father, and my daddy, sat at a round table in the kitchen to eat lunch. Dan Ellebracht was a big jovial man who ate the sausage and grits with gusto, all the while talking ranch business with Daddy.

"Gilbert, I think we need to clear some cedar in the back pasture. It's taking over."

Daddy nodded. "I'll take your word, Dan. Just give me a price first."

Years later, as Karl and Daniel were growing up, we visited the ranch several times a year, often with Mother and Daddy. By this time the land was leased to Arlis Zesch and later to my cousin Willard, neither of who lived there. Arlis did stay in the ranch house occasionally when he had several days of work to do. Evidently he enjoyed reading *Playboy* while there because Karl and Daniel found a stack of magazines on a shelf in the bathroom, much to their interest and my surprise.

The bathroom had a tub and lavatory but no toilet because there was no sewer. Wastewater ran through a pipe to the yard. So for a toilet we walked to the outhouse.

Most of the time the ranch house was ours to use. Bebbie and Opa would come and prepare the house first, bringing groceries, sheets, towels, and toilet paper. In the spring Bebbie always had wildflowers on the dining table. The only heat was a fireplace in the living room and the kitchen wood stove.

Karl and Daniel loved going to the ranch. To get there from Mason we turned off the highway to Junction onto a country road that ran through several other ranches. After unlocking the main gate, we passed through five gates with cattle guards.

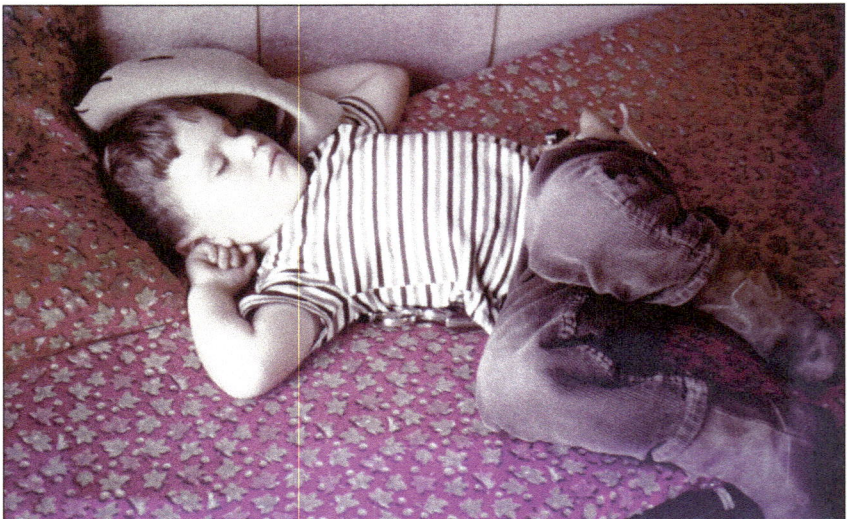

Little Cowboy Daniel

When Tom stopped at a gate, Karl said, "My turn," and jumped out of the car to open and close the gate. Then it was Daniel's turn. I think it made them feel like real ranchers in their cowboy hats and boots. But even cowboys get sleepy as Daniel did.

Our ranch was at the end of the road next to the Hoerster place. Their ranch house and ours shared a working windmill, another source of delight as well as water. Our house was a simple one-story frame building painted white. Tom designed a porch across the wall of the main entrance with slender cedar trunks for posts and a tin roof, which gave the house country character. Daddy had some locals pour the concrete and do the construction.

Ranch Music

On that porch we spent some memorable times. Tom and Karl played their guitar and ukulele. And during one visit we watched a total lunar eclipse through Opa's telescope. In a sky full of more stars than we ever saw in Austin, the moon looked like a ball instead of a glowing disk.

Another night, as we all sat on the porch, a rattlesnake slithered under Bebbie's chair without anyone seeing it approach. The porch was dark except for a shaft of light coming through the screen door.

Suddenly Opa said, "Vera ... get up slowly and move away. There's a rattlesnake coiled under your chair!"

Mother gasped and did so.

We all got up slowly, stepped inside, and looked out the screen door.

Tom and Opa searched for a weapon, but before they found anything the snake slithered away. From then on we looked under our chairs before sitting.

When we went on hikes we were always aware of the possibility of encountering a rattlesnake. That possibility became a reality when Tom, Karl, Daniel, Bonnie, and I were hiking along a road in the back pasture.

Karl stopped. "Look, a jackrabbit!"

We all stopped.

It sat on its haunches like a statue, ears turned toward us. At that moment we saw the rattlesnake, coiled, ready to strike the jackrabbit. Smart Bonnie sensed the danger and stayed close, maybe to protect us.

Karl put an arrow on his bow, fired at the snake, and missed but saved the life of the jackrabbit, who hopped away in giant leaps. The snake remained coiled, its tongue darting in and out.

"Kill it, kill it!" I yelled.

Picking up a rock, Tom threw it at the rattler. Then Karl, Daniel, and I threw rocks, lots of rocks. We became savages because in Texas if you see a rattlesnake, it is your duty to kill it. Which rock or rocks did the job we will never know, but together we killed that snake!

Tom found a long sturdy stick, picked up the dead snake, and carried it back to the ranch house. There he laid the rattler on the ground and pulled out the hunting knife he always carried in a sheath on his belt when we went hiking. He cut off the head and buried it.

"It could still poison someone," he said.

"Can we skin it and take it home?" Karl asked.

"You bet," Tom said.

As we all, Bebbie and Opa too, watched in awe, Tom turned the snake on its back and split the skin lengthwise, even as the body continued writhing. Then, holding the snake with one hand, he slowly peeled the skin from the flesh and cut the rattles off.

"Look," Daniel said, "its heart is still beating."

Karl and Billy

When it stopped, Tom hung the body over the barbed wire fence for some creature to devour during the night. The next morning the snake was gone, and we came home with a trophy, which Tom nailed to a rough cedar board. That mounted snakeskin has hung on one wall or another ever since. Recently Daniel gave it a coat of preservative and attached the rattles to the tail.

As this was a goat and sheep ranch, there were a lot of goats and a few sheep roaming around, and even fewer cattle. Opa, Karl, and Daniel liked feeding the goats mistletoe.

"I remember the sheep trying to reach mistletoe on the lower mesquite tree branches," Karl said recently. "That's where we came in."

One of the goats became a pet we named Billy. He was so tame that five-year-old Karl could straddle him and hold his horns.

There were two machines of the past abandoned on the ranch. One was an old wagon. Tom hooked it to our Rambler and pulled it near the ranch house. Karl and Daniel and sometimes friends we brought along used it as a set for cowboy play.

Ranch Wagon

The other machine was a broken down Model T that Opa assembled for Karl and Daniel. He knew how boys love cars, wagons and other large machinery.

Model T

We often hiked to the spring up in the hills, once with little Daniel riding in a Boy Scout pack on Tom's back! Sometimes Opa, Bebbie, and we drove up the road a way, parked, and hiked to the spring from there.

At the Spring

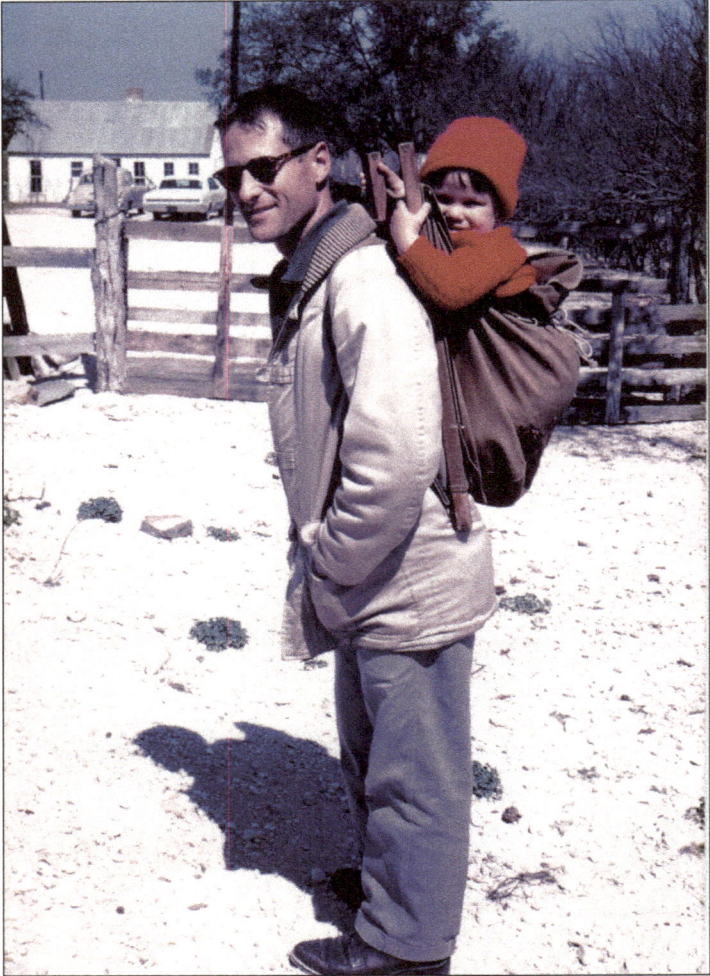

Tom Carrying Daniel

Bonnie loved taking hikes, always herding us along the way. As the boys grew older we invited friends like the Bergquist or Mather families to come with us. How we all stayed in that little ranch house, I don't know.

One time we took Brent and rode in Tom's Volkswagen Bug, Tom and I in the front seats, Karl and Brent in the back, and Daniel in the little compartment under the back window. On a hike Karl, Daniel, and Brent took turns shooting Karl's bow and arrows at trees and rocks, trying to see how far and how accurately they could send an arrow.

We knew that our ranch was once the Comanche's domain because of the many arrowheads Karl and Daniel found while we walked the land. It was a favorite pastime, and our boys had sharp eyes. Later on as I researched Comanches in Texas for writing the Texas Trilogy, I learned that the band that lived on our ranch called themselves the Penateka, or Honey Eaters. They were the band that made a treaty with German immigrants in 1847 that was never broken on either side. Otherwise we might not be here.

Karl Shoots an Arrow

During deer hunting season Opa leased the ranch to a group of hunters. They established a permanent campsite near the goat sheering shed. One of them was a beekeeper as well as a deer killer. He had bee-hives at their campground. In the summers he would bring us a frame of honeycomb, and Bebbie would scrape it off as Karl and Daniel watched. Karl says that is why he loves honey so much. He is a Honey Eater.

Bebbie and Honeycomb

We often spent Easter at the ranch with Bebbie and Opa. It could be rather chilly, an "Easter cold snap," as Bebbie called it, and we needed a fire in the fireplace and warm clothes. We dyed the eggs the night before, and Opa always went outside in the morning while we slept and played the Easter Bunny.

Before breakfast Karl and Daniel were out the door with their Easter baskets, searching for eggs. Opa was an ingenious bunny, hiding them in all sorts of places such as in a woodpile or behind a wagon wheel. The boys raced about seeing who could collect the most eggs. Opa often helped Daniel since he was at a disadvantage.

"Daniel, I think the Easter Bunny left one by the fence."

And Daniel would come running, the egg basket in hand. When he filled the basket, he showed it to Bebbie, who admired all the eggs he had found.

We didn't go to church at Easter. We went to the ranch. It was almost a holy place for us through the years, a place where the wind swept across the land, the stars were brilliant and unbelievably numerous, and where we led a different kind of life in the rocky, hilly landscape, far from civilization.

Bebbie and Daniel

8

Professor Tom and the Sixties

In 1959 Professor Roland Roessner invited Tom to teach in the UT School of Architecture. After much consideration, Tom decided to leave Fehr and Granger, become a professor, and start his own practice with Alan Taniguchi, who later became dean of the school.

Tom taught drawing and design. As Karl and Daniel got older, Tom enjoyed giving them the same drawing assignments that he gave his students and then took their drawings to class. The students thought someone in the class had done them, which amused Tom and made him proud.

Karl and Daniel became well acquainted with the campus. Tom and I would load a stroller and tricycle into our Rambler station wagon, drive to UT, and walk and ride around the campus. The boys loved picking Tom up after class. I parked in the slot by the back door of the architecture building and they would run in and find him, often with students in the lab still at work.

For his design classes, Tom took a unique approach. He had his students out on sites such as the playground for the Mental Health-Mental Retardation Day School. The students' task was to design and build a playground suited to the needs of these children. Instead of passively observing the children, Tom and his students led playground activities and encouraged the children to help them build the equipment.

Tom's favorite, most talented student was Ray Bailey, a country boy from Marshall, Texas, so talented that Tom hired him to work on projects that he was doing in his home studio. Ray's wife, Peggy was a devoted elementary school teacher and gave Karl and Daniel a copy of *Make Way for Ducklings* at Christmas.

One time when Ray was working with Tom, Karl came into the studio and said, "Tom, can we draw?"

Ray was impressed, not only that Karl wanted to draw with his dad, but that he called him Tom.

"Well," said Ray, "can I call you Tom, too?"

And from then on he did.

Tom being on the architecture faculty brought our family into a delightful group of friends, Bob and Jean Mather, Carl and Kate Bergquist, Richard and Gail Swallow, Bob and Sandy Harris, Alan and Leslie Taniguchi. These faculty members and their families became lifelong friends of ours.

When the Roosevelt Memorial Competition was announced in 1959, Tom, Bob Harris, and Richard Swallow decided to enter. The site was on the tidal basin in Washington D.C., alongside the cherry trees. They came up with a landscaped park with statues of Roosevelt, his colleagues, and the American people all around to show that he was a president of the people. Their proposal did not win but was published.

I had to laugh when I read that the winning proposal looked like a giant Stonehenge and was never built. Then came some enormous stone triangles by Marcel Breuer that never got erected either. Ironically, in 1969 President Johnson proclaimed that the site would be preserved as a park until a worthy design was found. Finally, landscape architect Lawrence Halprin proposed outdoor galleries set in a garden, which became a reality.

Once when Richard was working with Tom at our house, I invited him to share our simple lunch. We had not remodeled our house yet, so we dined in our breakfast room, a nook in the kitchen. One-year-old Karl sat in his highchair, not eating his yellow jello.

Boston-bred Richard looked at Karl and said, "Kahl, aren't you going to eat your jiggly jello?" With that Richard jiggled a spoonful and put it in his own mouth.

Karl grinned and then jiggled his jello and began to eat.

Not only did the faculty work together, our families socialized and partied at each other's homes. Sometimes our faculty parties included our children, so they became friends as well. Once we were invited to watch *The Wizard of Oz* at Bob and Sandy's house. Sandy, a gourmet cook, made pancakes in animal shapes for the children. And Kate did lovely pen and ink portraits of each child. Ours hang on the living/dining room wall.

We joined students at their parties and danced their dances, occasionally at the Vulcan Gas Company, a music hall on Congress Avenue that had a psychedelic light show accompanying loud rock music from a group called Shiva's Headband. Tom and I and our fellow faculty members danced along with the students. I felt a little self-conscious but danced anyway. One girl student came to me and said, "I admire your nerve." Whatever that meant. The Vulcan had no liquor license, did not allow marijuana, and seemed innocent to me. Karl remembers going with us one night.

Being in the University atmosphere inspired me to be more daring in my clothing style. One of Tom's students had a girlfriend who worked at a dress shop called Paraphernalia. Their clothes were unlike any others at the time. I was fascinated and began to shop there. One night they had a promotional party and I took Karl and Daniel, but the rock band was so loud that I feared for their ears.

My favorite purchase was a dress made of a black mesh fabric interwoven with silver threads. The dress reached mid-thigh, and I bought glittery silver hose to match and wore the outfit to a dance at a Texas Society of Architects convention in Houston. I was a hit.

That weekend our family stayed with Tom's sister, June Hensley, and her family in Friendswood. Later, Karl told me that while Tom and I were at the dance, June spanked Daniel for something. I was furious.

"Don't ever do that again," I told her, and she never did.

As my customer relationship with Paraphernalia grew, they asked me to be one of the models for a program on KLRU. I chose to wear a purple dress with geometric designs. As I walked before the camera, to my distress, they played the Beatles' song, "When I'm Sixty-Four." Yet I was only in my late thirties!

The 1960s were a turbulent time that turned brutal. Just before Thanksgiving Day of 1963, President Kennedy was assassinated in Dallas. The boys and I were there for the holidays, and Tom came the next day. Everyone remembers where they were and what they were doing at the time. It was a warm, sunny day. Bebbie, Opa, five-year-old Karl, one-year-old Daniel, and I were just finishing lunch in the breakfast room when the phone rang.

It was my brother Terry, calling from Tempe, Arizona, where he was a geography professor at the university.

"Do you know what's happening?" he asked. Of course we knew that President Kennedy and First Lady Jacqueline were in town campaigning for the next election, but the only TV was upstairs in what was a playroom for the boys.

"No, what?" Bebbie replied.

"The president has been shot while on a motorcade downtown," Terry said.

Bebbie repeated the news to us.

"Oh no!" I exclaimed, and we went upstairs to watch the news.

My parents were not Kennedy supporters, nor were they admirers of the first lady. Tom and I admired them both for their intelligence and cultured tastes, at least Jacqueline's, which seemed to rub off on Jack.

Karl did not understand the full gravity of the event. Yet he says he felt that "something was wrong." And Daniel understood little, if any, of the tragedy and went on playing with blocks as we watched the news. Karl stood transfixed, looking at the TV screen and at our reactions.

"Come, Karl," I said.

He climbed onto the couch beside me and I wrapped my arm around him and tried to explain.

"Somebody shot President Kennedy but we're safe."

"Why?" he asked.

"Because that person hated him."

"Why?"

"I don't know, Karl, but we're safe. Don't worry."

He put his head against my shoulder, and I cuddled him as the news played on. When Daniel noticed the loving, he climbed up too. Such innocents. Even Oswald was once an innocent, and I wondered what happened to turn him into a killer.

Three years later, on a blazing hot day in August of 1966, another violent act occurred, partly visible from our back porch. Karl was eight and Daniel was four. The boys and I had just arrived home from the washateria when Mrs. Joseph's maid came across the street and told us what was happening.

"Somebody is shooting people from the UT tower!"

"Oh, my God!" I said.

Tom was teaching a class, and I knew that his lab on the second floor had windows facing the tower. We hurried inside and turned on the radio because we had no TV then.

"Is he going to shoot Tom?" Karl asked.

"No, I'm sure Tom will be careful," I said, but I wasn't sure.

After trying to call the school office, the boys and I went downstairs to our back porch where we had a view of the tower. We could see puffs of smoke coming from the top.

Karl remembers being afraid he might shoot *us*, which wasn't far from the truth since Whitman had a scoped high-powered rifle and we lived less than a mile from campus.

We had no idea where Tom was or if he was okay until he finally walked in several hours later. There were no cell phones back then.

We rushed to hug him and hold on to him as if he had just come back from the dead.

"Oh, Tom, we were so worried!" I said.

"Sorry I didn't call to let you know, but there were no phones available so I just decided to walk home."

"Tell us what happened."

"Well, I was in the design lab when the shooting started. We all rushed to the windows to see what was happening."

I gasped. "Are you crazy?"

"Then cops came running into the lab, cleared everyone out, and started shooting up at the tower with their little pea shooter pistols."

Karl remembers the story as Tom continued to tell it:

"Meanwhile my dad, a youthful forty at the time, went out the back of the building and ran along behind some bushes to get a better view, no less — young and foolish. A woman was shot right in front of him on the south plaza."

I was aghast but grateful that Tom was safely at home. The event came to be known as the Tower Sniper.

The violence caught on. In 1968 Martin Luther King was assassinated, which brought on more protests against racial inequality. Then only two months later Robert Kennedy was shot and killed as he campaigned for the presidency. The world seemed to be going mad, especially in America and Vietnam where we were fighting someone else's war and an obscene number of our soldiers were being killed. All of these horrible happenings brought on protests, people marching in the streets of cities all over the country, especially students, protesting the war and the draft. Some of the protests turned violent with police clubbing, tear-gassing, and even killing protestors. Chaos.

At UT there was an active chapter of the Students for a Democratic Society. Tom, along with Alan Taniguchi and other faculty members, marched with the students but fortunately none of their protests turned violent.

In 1969 this group also protested the UT administration order to cut down forty mature trees along Waller Creek on the campus in order to expand the football stadium. Students chained themselves to the trees or sat on the branches. Tom and Dean Alan joined them to make sure no one was hurt. Eventually the students were forced to come down by police with billy clubs and bulldozers. Football won over nature. It was reported that the president of the Board of Regents clapped his hands as each tree fell and said, "I'm disturbed that a bunch of dirty nothings can disrupt the workings of a great university in the name of academic freedom." Substitute *football team* for *university*.

Later, students dragged tree limbs to the South Mall and piled them on the steps. They also planted new trees and grass along the creek. Of course, Karl and Daniel only heard about this from Tom, but I have no doubt that his actions had an influence in bringing up our boys.

Increasingly Tom became interested in urban renewal and served on many Austin planning committees. In 1968 the City of Austin hired Tom and fellow architectural professor Bob Harris to develop a plan for Congress Avenue and East 6th Street. In an interview with the Austin History Center Tom said:

"On Congress Avenue we changed the parking arrangement to head-in parking between islands with trees planted in them. It was a whole new street design without making the traffic lanes narrower. And, of course, we changed the light fixtures and installed benches. So that was one of my favorite urban design projects, I think."

The Shefelman and Harris plan was finally implemented in 1975.

This was the era of the Beatles who freed young people to resist authority generation after generation and still do. Little did I know at the time how much they affected our sons. Karl wrote in his memoir:

"In the summer of '67 the Beatles' *Sgt. Pepper* album came out. I was nine at the time. I'm pretty sure my mom bought it for me that same year. I remember being at Bill Bergquist's house, whose mom had also bought him the album. I remember both our moms standing in the living room chatting with each other about the Beatles, probably while we were all listening to the album. I swear to this day that one of our moms, probably mine, in her charmingly naive way, said something along the lines of 'You know, I don't think the Beatles' music is as drug oriented as some of the others.'

"At any rate, in the following few years, I listened to that album over and over, totally wore it out. Despite what it meant to the teenager or young adult of the era, that music opened a whole new world of child-like imagination for me as a young boy."

I'm so glad I bought the album for Karl and Daniel. It seems to have helped make them the creative men they are. I also gave them classical music recordings made for children.

The 60s ended with the magnificent accomplishment of sending two astronauts to the moon. By this time we had a TV. Tom, Karl, and I were watching the landing of the spacecraft. Daniel and John were playing outside, and I called them in to see the historic event. They were only five years old and preferred to play. So the three of us watched as Neil Armstrong stepped onto the moon's surface, saying these unforgettable words:

"That's one small step for man, one giant leap for mankind."

9

Cousins and Holidays

I remember the joy of growing up with my cousins and wanted Karl and Daniel to have the same experience. So we traveled to Friendswood and Dallas whenever we could.

Friendswood, where the Hensleys lived, was the favorite cousin place. June and her husband Jack, nicknamed Switch, had several acres of land, including a pond, rental space at the entrance area for a half-dozen trailer homes, a barn, and a sprawling house at the rear of the property. The cousins, Laura, Brent, and Charley, loved to swim and fish in the pond.

Fishing in Friendswood

June ran the place while Switch worked as a civil engineer. He and his dad, Carl, joined in making property investments and often lost money. I never understood what they did but a few times they tried to get Tom interested. Fortunately Harold, Tom's dad, advised him not to become involved.

June and Switch seemed to resent my cultural tastes. Maybe I seemed arrogant and judgmental, which I can be. I was not interested in football or in reliving my college days like they were. I loved classical music and Tolstoy novels and Shakespeare plays. Still, Switch did not entirely reject my ways and at times was attracted to my difference. I think he was not entirely devoted to June the way Tom was devoted to me.

The cousins were not judgmental and loved being together. They swam, fished, tossed a football, and played with the dachshunds, Donya and Rye, who were sweet dogs. Charley had a pet raccoon, who was not always sweet, especially when Switch tried to put him outdoors and got bitten.

I remember one evening when Brent brought in a Bill Cosby record. Although Cosby has a bad name now, then he was known for his monologues about growing up with his little brother Russell. It was my first time to hear his routine, and all of us laughed until we were breathless.

Aside from hamburgers and steak that Switch cooked outdoors, seafood was the specialty in the Hensley home, especially fresh boiled shrimp in the shell with homemade cocktail sauce. It was also a specialty at Aunt Lucy's house. She was Switch's aunt who lived alone in a house on stilts on Galveston Bay. She had a pier where the cousins fished for crabs with chicken necks on long strings and caught them.

Lucy dropped their catch live into a big kettle of boiling water on the stove. One time Laura came running into the living room.

"They're climbing out of the pot!"

We all rushed to the kitchen. Sure enough, the crabs were crawling all over the floor, desperately trying to escape. Fortunately all were caught and returned to their watery hell.

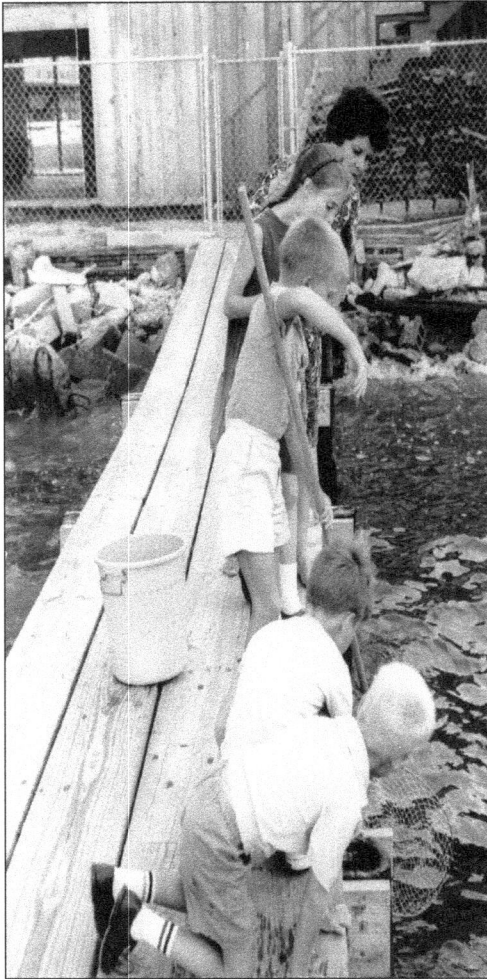

Fishing for Crab

Now for the Jordan side of the family. My brother Terry and his wife Marlis, and their three children, Tina, Sonya, and Eric, lived in Denton where Terry taught geography at North Texas State University. We traditionally had Thanksgiving dinner at one of our homes, either at Bebbie and Opa's, which was the best, at Marlis and Terry's house in Denton, or at our house. Of course, Bebbie was the best cook of all, and Karl and Daniel loved being in her house. It was a second home to them, and Bebbie and Opa second parents.

We women, Mother, Marlis, and I shared the preparation, though Mother was always in charge. She knew how she wanted everything to be, and Marlis and I followed her directions.

Meanwhile, the children amused themselves outdoors in good weather. When they were younger, they rode the resident tricycle and little wagon up and down the neighborhood sidewalk. Later Tom, Terry, and the children played basketball in the driveway or threw a football in the front yard and front yards of the neighbors.

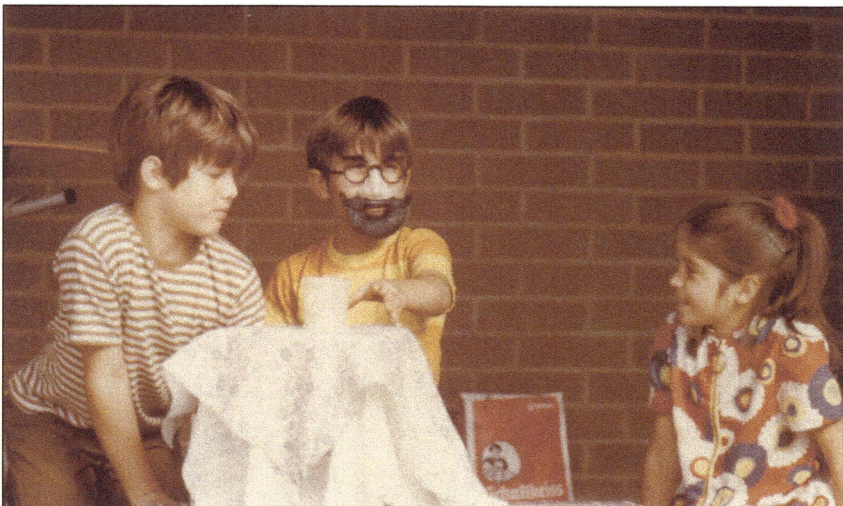

Magic Show

At last the turkey arrived on the table along with Bebbie's moist cornbread dressing made from scratch, as was every dish, cranberry

89

sauce, mashed sweet potatoes, green beans, and a platter of raw veggies. Later came pumpkin pie with vanilla ice cream.

One Thanksgiving at Terry's house, the children put on a circus for the adults. Daniel wore round glasses and a beard and did a magic show with Karl. Little Sonya wore a clown costume, and Karl held a hoop for her to run through. Creative kids!

Cousin Circus

Christmas was sometimes at Bebbie and Opa's house, especially when the boys were quite young. Karl's first Christmas was there, and among other things he got a baby walker. He could sit in a little sling and zip around using his legs. Daniel's first Christmas was also at Bebbie and Opa's and he got the same baby walker, all shined up like new. He didn't know the difference. But Daniel *did* know the difference when he got Karl's red recycled bicycle for his sixth birthday. He was mad because he wanted a cool spider bike. Still, a little brother has something a big brother doesn't, a playmate.

Karl's First Christmas

I loved celebrating at our house, too. We always placed the Christmas tree in the living room where it could be seen from the top of the stairs. Once we cut a cedar tree at the ranch and brought it home. Usually we purchased a fir tree at the Optimist Club lot on Lamar. In my romanticized vision of Christmas, I decided one year, 1968, that we should walk there and carry the tree home by hand as if coming in from the forest. With John Newman's help we did.

Except for stringing the lights, decorating the tree was an event we all cherished. Every year we added a few ornaments and every year we took them out of the box, remembering where each came from. Tom and I had bought an assortment of shiny red, blue, and gold balls before Karl and Daniel came along. Then I let the boys each choose an ornament to add. One year they both chose nesting balls we found at Scarbrough's department store downtown, made in Germany and painted with Christmas scenes. They also made decorations at school, the most memorable one being from Karl's kindergarten, a toilet paper roll painted gold. The children painted and decorated toilet paper rolls and thread spools as well as paper angels and birds sprinkled with glitter. We still have them. Bebbie made embroidered felt ornaments, including Rudolph the Red-Nosed Reindeer and our dachshund Schotzie. Aunt Mae crocheted snowflakes for us, and Mrs. Joseph across the street made miniature stockings dotted with sequins for our tree.

Sometimes there were different opinions about where something should hang. Daniel had a penchant for hanging ornaments from the tinsel, which neither Karl nor I liked.

Karl said, "Don't hang it from the tinsel, Daniel. It looks weird."

"I like it," Daniel said, and so it stayed.

We have a family tradition about opening presents on Christmas morning, one person, one gift at a time. It was my idea to prolong the joy and let everyone fully appreciate each gift as it was unwrapped. If Tom received a book, he became lost in reading until it was his turn to open another present. As for Karl and Daniel, they wanted to open one after another and then play with their toys or read their books. Still, they kept the tradition and now love to tease me about it, although I think they appreciate the value of slowing down the process.

Another tradition was making and decorating Christmas cookies, which came from my family and Daddy's German heritage. I used Mother's recipe, and rolled out the dough. The boys and sometimes friends would cut them out in all the cookie cutter shapes we had and then decorate them with different colors of sugar, red dots, and silver balls.

Sometimes Harold (Granddad) flew down from Seattle for Christmas, either at our house or Bebbie and Opa's. When Karl and Daniel were little, they thought he lived in the sky! Harold always stayed in a hotel, which I did not understand at the time. Why wouldn't he want to stay with family? Now I do understand. He wanted time alone. Also he often had trouble sleeping and liked to roam about.

Tom's mother, Madolene, took her own life while we were traveling around the world. Eventually Harold married again, a blond woman named Sylvia, who had emotional and health problems. Though she seemed to love Karl and Daniel and always brought them cute clothes and their first Lego blocks, she made life difficult for Harold. He had a way of being attracted to beautiful women with problems, and it was a relief when they divorced.

Finally he chose the right woman, Nona Church, Tom and June's "mother across the street," who was by then a widow. She was traveling with friends in the South Pacific when Harold realized how much he missed her company. He called her all the way across the ocean, proposed, and she said yes. The whole family gathered in Seattle for their wedding and celebration in August of 1977. Two families linked once more. All was right with the world.

Christmas Cookies

Granddad Visits

Christmas 1968

10

Skiing in a Winter Wonderland

Since Tom and I met while skiing, we wanted our boys to learn how to ski and enjoy a winter wonderland. Our first trip was to Santa Fe during the Christmas holidays of 1965. We stayed in the Bishop's Lodge in the foothills above the town. I had stayed there with a group of college friends on my first ski trip before I met Tom. Like all buildings in the historic area, Bishop's Lodge is adobe style but on a grand scale.

We had a big room with plenty of space for Karl and Daniel to play with their new set of Lego blocks. Every night our beds were turned down and chocolate mints placed on our pillows, a luxury we had never experienced before. The lobby felt more like a living room with a heavy beamed ceiling, Navajo rugs, couches, lounge chairs, fireplace, and a Christmas tree.

There was plenty of snow that year so Tom and the boys made two snowmen on the lodge grounds.

The ski basin was a thirty-minute drive up into the mountains from the lodge. Even though Tom was an excellent driver on snowy roads, there were times when the drive got scary on turns, especially if another car came from the opposite direction and we were on the outside edge near the abyss.

Karl had his first ski lessons but I did not like the instructor. When his young students fell, he was not helpful or encouraging. Still, Karl learned how to snowplow. Tom and I took turns skiing and playing with Daniel.

Snowmen in Santa Fe

For the next three years we opted for Cloudcroft, New Mexico, instead. On the way we stopped and picked bouquets of dried plants along the highway and brought them home. Because this drive was more southerly, there was no snow in the dry, flat lowlands or even in the foothills of the Sacramento Mountains. We would always worry whether there was snow for skiing and playing.

"I see snow!" one of us shouted as the road climbed higher and higher, just before arriving at Cloudcroft. The town's name means pasture for the clouds. On arriving it seemed a miracle that the pasture was covered in deep snow.

We stayed in The Lodge, a grand old hotel rebuilt after a fire in 1909. I remember the giant fireplace in the spacious lobby and the feeling of being welcome there. The boys also remember the pinball game room just off the lobby. Behind the hotel there was a gentle slope where we played in the snow and rode in a snowmobile.

Best of all, the ski school employed great instructors. Daniel bonded with his teacher and trusted him. The beginner's slope had a rope tow up the hill, and there Daniel learned how to snowplow, with his instructor doing a backward snowplow in front of him.

The Lodge

By the time we decided to try Taos in 1970, both boys were good skiers, and Tom and I were getting better too. Tom would try almost any slope and somehow get down it. I remember once when we were all coming down the final zigzag road to the bottom, Tom cut off the road and just plunged down the mountain — terrible form but he made it.

Every year I worried that one of us would break a limb but we never did. Though one year when the boys were adults living in New York, Daniel broke his leg playing basketball in a park right before we all met in Taos. He came anyway and enjoyed telling girls in the St. Bernard Hotel bar that he broke his leg skiing Al's Run, an expert slope that is more cliff than slope.

Taos Ski Valley is a real family place with a quaint alpine village and simple nightlife, all in walking distance. We always stayed in the Sierra del Sol. It was situated across a creek from the ski headquarters and lodge. We liked the separation from the chair lift area made by snow-covered pines and fir trees along the creek. All we had to do was cross a little wooden bridge to get there.

Usually we rented a second floor condominium with a high-pitched ceiling, a spacious living and dining area, and a balcony overlooking the creek. Big, beautiful mountain jays came to eat the crumbs we put on the railing. We had a view of the famously difficult Al's Run looming above, enough to scare beginners at first sight but inspiring to watch an occasional expert manage with grace. I believe that Tom, Karl, and Daniel eventually took the Al's Run challenge, unbeknownst to me.

The Shefelmen in Cloudcroft

The fireplace was a black stove with a hood and tall interior chimney that heated the whole room. The management supplied piñon pine wood, which has a distinctive smell when it burns and always reminds me of Taos. We loved that black stove so much that when Tom designed our second house, he specified the same one. A guest once said, "This looks like a ski lodge." Exactly.

Ernie Blake, originally Ernst Bloch, the Swiss founder and owner of the Taos Ski Valley ran an excellent ski school. It had the reputation of being the best in the country and rightly so. Not only did Ernie demand the best from his instructors, he stashed pitchers of martinis in tree wells around the mountain.

We rented skis and lined up for class on the beginner's slope. People demonstrated their skills and were assigned to instructors. Tom and Karl were assigned to a more advanced class, Daniel and I to different intermediate levels. My class of adults did stop for a martini after we had negotiated a steep slope.

We also took private lessons, again Tom and Karl together for a time, Karl with perfect coordination and Tom with his own daring style. I believe they bonded man-to-man during those lessons. Later Tom and I had a private lesson together. I was far more conservative than he and did not like to ski at great speed. Realizing this, our instructor demonstrated parallel turns in slow motion with exaggerated movements, and helped me finally get the feel of lifting and shifting my weight onto the downhill ski. It was a revelation. Meanwhile Daniel had lessons with Ken, a tall, lovable guy, whom Daniel requested each year.

On a very cold, windy, snowy day I happened to be at the top of that long zigzag road, shivering in the biting wind when Daniel and Ken appeared. I was aghast. Daniel was only eight years old.

"Why did you bring him up here on such a cold day?" I asked.

"He's doing just fine," Ken said. "He's a tough little kid."

Daniel grinned at me. His goggles were so big that they covered his face except for his nose and mouth.

Our Austin friends, the Swallows, began coming to Taos as well. We sometimes joined Richard and Gail and their daughters, Caryn, Susan, and Linda after a day of skiing. They owned their skis and had matching ski outfits with a swallow emblem on their jackets. Gail came from a wealthy family, and Richard designed and built a tower-like second home for them in the ski valley. It had a circular stairway from the ground floor to the third floor. We could not afford to build a house there or even buy our own skis, but since we only skied once a year that idea was not a priority. Besides, we loved the Sierra del Sol.

Linda, the youngest daughter, was pretty and popular at Austin High, and Daniel had a secret crush on her. One evening the Swallow family visited us. The only problem was that Daniel was suffering from altitude sickness and stayed in the bedroom. Or was it lovesickness?

Then came the year a blizzard blew in, highways were closed, and our Rambler broke down as we were driving home. Fortunately we reached Santa Fe and La Fonda, the historic pink adobe-style hotel on the square. Since many travelers were stranded, the hotel only had a luxury suite left, which they let us have for a regular room rate. It was glorious. After a spicy New Mexican meal, Karl and Daniel turned on the large TV and flung themselves down on the carpet to watch. School started the next day, but I was the only one concerned.

Tom and I went out into the snow-covered square. The snow had stopped, there were no people, no cars, just an otherworldly quiet. As we stood there in awe, the bell in the cathedral at the corner of the square began to toll. We were caught in an eternal moment.

One year Karl invited his best friend, Charles Larkam, to go with us, his first ski trip. The two were teenagers at the time. Charles, as is his way, was excited and adaptable to whatever came. The night we arrived, he and Karl carried firewood up the back stairs, trip after trip. The altitude of the ski valley is 9200 feet, and we had not yet acclimated. That night Charles got sick and was throwing up.

Concerned, Tom went to the bathroom door. "Are you all right, Charles?"

"Oh yes, I'm fine," he answered in typical Charles fashion.

And the next day he was.

During Christmas of 1973 there was not enough snow for downhill skiing so we tried cross-country. The four of us set out through the vast wilderness surrounding the Taos ski valley with a map. Thanks should go to Ernie Blake for purchasing so much land and for refusing to let a highway be cut from the valley to the Red River ski area on the other side of the mountains.

Cross-country skiing is more like hiking than skiing. No thrilling descent down a mountain, just the quiet magic of a snow-covered wilderness where chipmunks scrambled across the snow.

Igloo

We made the best of the lack of snow. The pond, fed by the creek in front of the Sierra del Sol, was frozen solid. We rented ice skates and tried that sport as well. But the most awe-inspiring activity was building an igloo. There was enough snow for Tom, Karl, and Daniel to make blocks of it by packing cardboard boxes one after another and constructing a life-size igloo with an arched doorway they could crawl through. It was yet another time that Tom and our sons made something together with their hands.

Karl, Mom, and Daniel Off to Ski Lessons

11

California, Here We Come

*I*n the summer of 1969 we took Karl and Daniel to California, then up to Washington State to see where Granddad lived. During the flight to Los Angeles, the attendants served us breakfast crepes with fresh strawberries and maple syrup. At the time Continental called its planes Proud Birds. Flying was a joyous adventure then. Imagine!

Where do you go first in California if you have children? Disneyland, of course. In LA we rented a sporty white Camaro and drove to the Disneyland Hotel, set in a lush tropical garden within walking distance of the amusement park.

As we entered the elevator, seven-year-old Daniel said to the occupants, "This is our first big trip." Indeed it was and his enthusiasm was contagious.

Karl took hundreds of photos as we walked around the park. Looking at them now, I remember what a fantasy it is, not only for children but also for parents. The first monorail in America, the tree house restaurant, the miniature thatch-roofed cottages for make-believe creatures, a giant whale with open mouth on a waterway for boats to go in and, hopefully, out, a horse-drawn streetcar, and a paddle wheel river boat, all made me feel like a child again. I think that is Disney's key to success.

Nothing else in Los Angeles could compare. From there we drove up the coast on Highway 1, stopping in Santa Barbara for a swim in the ocean. Then on to San Luis Obispo where we stayed at the Madonna

Inn, a quirky hotel with every room decorated in a different theme, such as Caveman, Rock Bottom, or Cloud Nine. Strangely I cannot remember the theme of ours but I think it had something to do with boulders that made up one wall.

I vividly remember an incident that occurred in the dining room that evening. Tom and I sometimes let Karl and Daniel have a sip of our wine or beer. When we did so at the Madonna Inn, a manager hopped on us.

"You can't do that here! We could lose our license."

It was so abrupt that I started crying.

"I'm so sorry, Madam," he said and departed.

In a moment he returned bearing gifts of chocolate candy.

"May this make up for my intrusion."

And it did. Funny what one remembers, often because of the degree of emotion involved.

The next morning we drove on to the Monterrey Peninsula and stayed in Carmel-by-the-Sea. At every restaurant Daniel ordered the same dish, the most expensive item on the menu.

"Abalone," he said, pleased with himself.

This new love started from finding and picking up luminous abalone shells and wondering what once lived inside. Daniel was not an adventurous eater like his big brother. Karl loved raw oysters so much that he was willing to take a tin of smoked oysters to school for lunch and endure his friends holding their noses and saying "Eeewww!"

Not Daniel, not until abalone.

We were now in Big Sur. Stopping at a place where rock outcroppings led down to the ocean, we walked around on the flat top area, watching the waves slam into the rocks and spray high in the air. Suddenly I realized that Karl and Daniel were nowhere in sight. I panicked as Tom and I searched.

"Karl! Daniel! Where are you?" we called, but the waves hitting the rocks drowned out our voices and hopefully theirs.

Had they been swept away into the ocean?

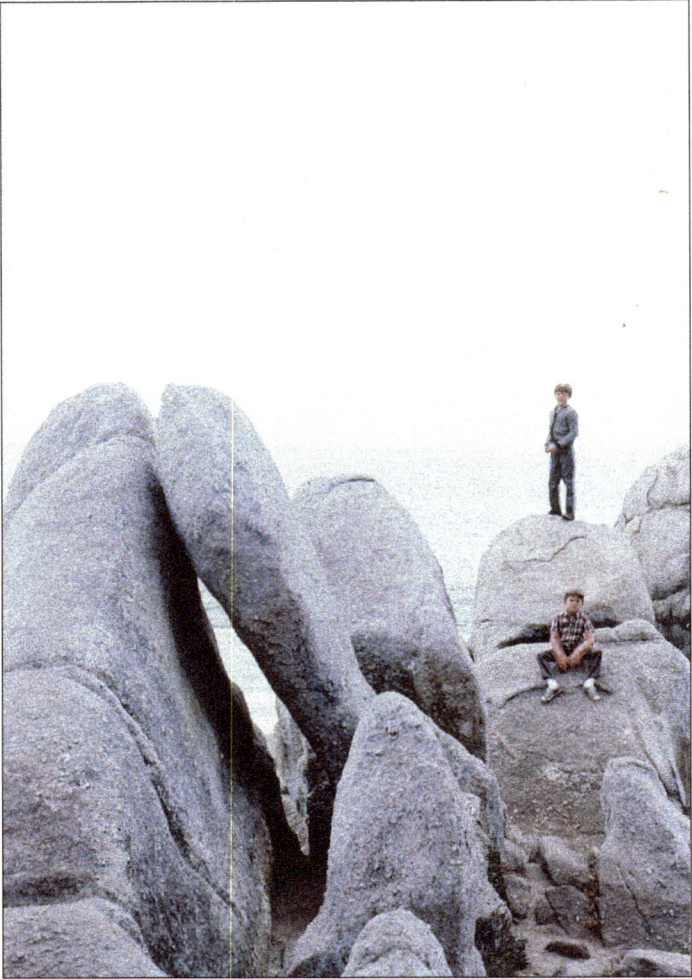

Monterrey Peninsula

106

No, thank God, Tom found both boys climbing around on the rocks, unaware of our distress.

He shepherded them up to the top saying, "Never, never leave our sight in a place like this!"

All I could do was hug them.

At another stop along the peninsula, Karl wanted to climb on a cliff and I said, "No."

Frustrated, he said, "Mom, you're a queer," with no idea of what the word meant. Some hippies sitting nearby were amused.

Then on to San Francisco and the donut-shaped hotel near Fisherman's Wharf. Karl and Daniel loved staying in hotels and playing "Spy and Go Seek." Wise or not, we let them have the run of the place, literally. They rode the elevators, ran around the halls, and hid from each other. The management never complained.

Other than hotel fun, we did what tourists do — walked Fisherman's Wharf, rode the cable cars, and visited Chinatown and the Golden Gate Park.

After a few days we climbed in our little sporty car, crossed the Golden Gate Bridge, and headed north for 100 miles to Sea Ranch. Tom knew about this community because of its planning and architecture, and had admired it from afar. One of the architects, Charles Moore, later became a partner with Tom on the design competition for a new Austin City Hall. They won first place but did not get the job. Charles had a strong influence on Tom's architecture. Tom designed our second home in a similar style of unpainted cedar and shed roofs. It sat on posts made from telephone poles so as not to disturb the sloping wooded site. Tom called it a "shedifice."

Sea Ranch is the perfect name because this community was once a sheep ranch and the property runs along the edge of the sea for ten miles. The sheep are still there to keep the grass cut. Planners and architects developed a community of homes designed to make a minimal impact on the dramatic landscape.

We stayed in The Lodge and had a view of the Pacific below and out to the horizon. A path led down to the rocky edge of the sea, where we found tidal pools with living starfish and sea urchins.

"Come look!" Daniel called. He had found a large sea urchin shell, which we packed carefully and brought home, along with all the abalone shells.

Then it was time to say farewell to California and head up to Seattle. We drove back to San Francisco, stopping in the Redwood National Park on the way, and flew to Seattle.

Granddad met us at the airport. After hugging Karl and Daniel, he said, "You see, boys, I don't live in the sky."

No, he lived alone in an apartment and put us up at a hotel in downtown Seattle, near the waterfront and Pike Place Market. The boys loved watching the fishmongers toss a whole salmon to another employee to be wrapped. Part of the charm of this market is that people who work there seem to enjoy it. Thus, so do the visitors.

When Tom was growing up, the Italian owner of the market, Joe Desimone, was a client of Harold's law firm. Every Thanksgiving Joe appeared at the Shefelmans' door with a turkey and bottle of wine.

"Eat-ah your turkey and drink-ah your wine," Tom remembers he always said as he handed them over.

Harold, a prominent lawyer and civic leader, was on the Planning Commission for Seattle's 1962 World's Fair and helped it remain a civic center. He championed Minoru Yamasaki as architect for the Science Center and became lifelong friends with "Yama" and his wife Teruko or "Terri."

Though the Science Center is graceful, it is the iconic Space Needle that became the symbol of Seattle and the World's Fair. It was a treat when Harold took us to dinner in the revolving spaceship that sits atop the 500-foot tripod. Because of Harold's reputation, we had a prime table at the outer edge. Karl and Daniel had fun putting objects on the revolving part of the windowsill and watching for them to come around again.

"Look, here's the pen!" Karl exclaimed.

Whatever we had for dinner could not rival the view of Seattle, the Puget Sound, and Mt. Rainier, our next adventure.

During this first visit to Seattle, Granddad and we hiked a trail that led from Paradise Inn to the ice caves. We passed through meadows of wildflowers and crossed streams where we stopped to drink the icy water. There were chipmunks galore, darting here and there, a deer looking at us with big wary eyes, and furry marmots. One stood on his hind legs eating lupine blooms and sniffing the air. When we stopped to watch, he ran to a nearby flat rock and lay on his belly, keeping an eye on us.

As we climbed above the tree line the thick edge of the glacier came into view with its gaping holes of the caves. Entering them was an eerie experience. The arched ceiling of pocked ice lit by the afternoon sun made it seem as if we were on another planet. Unfortunately the ice caves are gone now, victim of global warming. The ice melted and the glacier receded. Will it ever advance again?

We ended our stay by riding a Washington State Ferry from Seattle, across the Strait of Juan de Fuca to Victoria, British Columbia. There we stayed in the Empress Hotel at Granddad's expense, even though he was not with us. It overlooks the inner harbor in regal Victorian splendor. Karl and Daniel played "Spy and Go Seek" in the maze garden, a perfect place for their game.

Now back to our life in Austin.

12

Architect Tom

*T*om loved teaching but he was eager to get back into architectural practice. Charley Granger called professors who also practiced "subsidized bastards." No matter. It was Tom's way into establishing a firm with Alan Taniguchi. They first rented a small house on 15th Street near Lavaca and hired former student Walter Vackar to hold down the office.

As the firm began to draw clients, Tom and Alan made Walter a partner and David Minter joined as a fourth, so it became Taniguchi, Shefelman, Vackar, Minter or TSVM. They decided to purchase a historic building on Congress Avenue at 3rd Street, across from the old train station. The building was once a hotel for travelers and sometimes prostitutes.

They leased the first floor to a glass company and gutted the second floor for their office, adding a new stairwell and creating a huge open space with a high ceiling of stamped tin. The existing tall arched windows allowed the space to be filled with light. The open space was lined with rows of drafting tables. Karl and Daniel loved visiting this office and sitting at a drafting table to make their own drawings alongside Tom.

Tom's favorite projects were those when he was directly involved with people, not corporations, whether it be the homeowners or a church building committee or a city planning commission. Of course, a lot of the joy depended on the client, but even the most difficult could not resist Tom's talent, warmth, and humor.

Daniel in Tom's Office

When asked how he began the design process, he replied, "With conferences and sketches with clients. I am known for being able to sketch upside down for a client sitting across the table."

Tom was a good listener and knew how to translate what he heard into art. He once said, "Architects are reproached for being concerned with form and yet not in tune with the needs of people." This attitude is exactly what he strove to avoid by listening carefully to his clients.

Bill and Mary Kay McLean commissioned Tom to design their house on Mesa Drive because he listened. As the three of them stood on the site together for the first time, Tom's first question was, "What do you envision here?"

"I hired him on the spot," Bill said.

As more work came in, TSVM hired more architects. One of those employees, Ed Lee, spoke at Tom's memorial service about working at TSVM. Since I never worked alongside Tom at his office, Ed's description is dear to me.

He stepped up to the podium, his face sweet with a smile, his hair thick and gray, and this is what he said in his gentle but manly voice.

"I can remember my first day at TSVM. I sat near Walter and across the aisle from Tom. I can remember sitting there and thinking I'd died and gone to heaven, 'cause there I was next to Tom, one of my heroes.

"I remember that Tom's method of work just totally flabbergasted me. As he was designing a space, unlike most architects, he would get to the end of a schematic design, and then he would start this huge perspective of the main space in the building and he, what I call, 'went under' for a couple of days, just with an immense concentration, drawing that perspective of the space. And after maybe three days working eight or ten hours a day on that project and saying very little, he would kind of come up for a breath.

"Sometimes I went over to look and he would say, 'What do you think?'

"And I said, 'Well, it's beautiful, Tom.'

"And he said, 'Yeah, but I think this space needs to be about two feet longer and the slope of the ceiling needs to come down from four and twelve to three and twelve. Then I think it would really work.'

"I just looked at him and said, 'I think that may be right.'

"He would start again, altering the drawing that he'd spent three or four days to the new specifications that he thought would work better, and sure enough, it would come out exactly like he had intended.

"Tom had an amazing ability to concentrate and focus that I've never witnessed in another person or another architecture office in my life. And he taught me that. He taught me how to go inside myself and find the way that the space wanted to be. And until I found that, to kind of not give up."

Thank you, Ed.

I believe Tom also taught these skills to Karl and Daniel by example when they visited his office or when he worked in his home studio. They saw that one could make a living by drawing.

Sometimes he took the boys along when he was supervising construction. One of their favorite projects was Inner Space Cavern near Georgetown. Tom designed an administration building for the owner.

Of course, Karl and Daniel were proud to be the sons of the architect, but more exciting was the chance to go into the cavern even before it was open to the public. The owner generously allowed the boys to pick up a few pieces of stalactites and stalagmites for their rock collections. A rare privilege for these two rock lovers.

The experience also gave Karl a fascination with caves. Later he and some high school friends decided to explore a cave south of Austin. I knew nothing about it until afterward. They entered and made their way through some extremely tight spaces. Coming out, Karl and the other boys suffered claustrophobic panic but managed somehow to control it. Bringing up boys can be scary at times.

Another favorite Tom project was a home and studio that he designed for Ishmael Soto and family near Eanes Elementary School. Ishmael's son, Bud, was the same age as Karl and they played together as Ishmael and helpers constructed the house themselves. He was a well-known ceramic artist, and paid Tom's architectural fee in pots and sculpture.

The pot that lives in our hearts is a lamp Tom designed and Ishmael made to hang from an old rusty chain over our dining table. The outside glaze is mottled dark blue and black, the interior a pale bluish-gray. The pot is pierced with holes that allow light to form patterns on the ceiling. A sacred lamp that has witnessed countless family meals and is part of our lives. It has moved with us two times and will never be left behind, even though we almost did so twice. It was Karl and Daniel who demanded that it belonged to our family in spite of the fact that it was attached to the ceiling. A testimony to the icon it had become and to what family gathering at the table meant for all of us. My own upbringing inspired this gathering for meals.

Ishmael also agreed to give pottery lessons to our boys as part of the architectural fee. He was on the UT art school faculty and taught in his home studio. If the fee had been paid in money, it would be long gone. Instead, I have the pots Karl and Daniel made under his instruction. They are precious to me and remain in use.

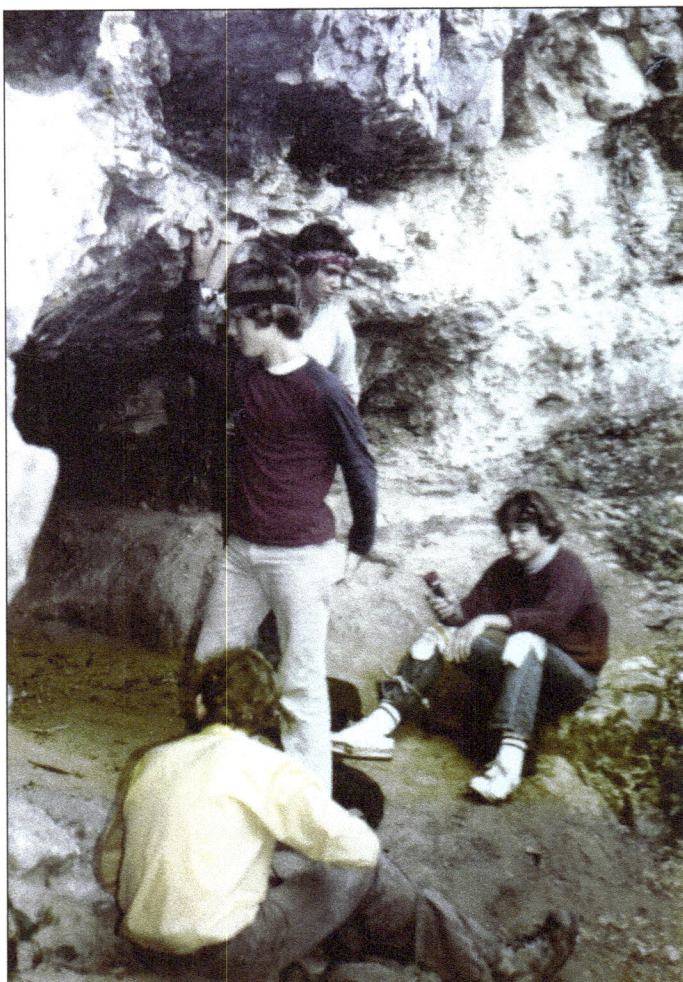

Karl Standing in Front of Cave

Karl remembers the college girls in the class who all seemed to love Ishmael and vice versa. One time we asked Walter Vackar to take Karl to pottery lessons when neither of us could. Walter, wearing Hollywood dark glasses, picked Karl up in a sporty convertible, impressing him and the girls who surrounded them upon arrival. Karl felt cool to be with such a guy in such a car surrounded by beautiful college girls.

Another residence with ideal clients was *Waldheim*, Forest Home, which he designed for Waldi and Harley Browning. It, too, won an Austin Chapter AIA Honor Award. As was often true, we became good friends, and the boys often visited the site when Tom was supervising construction.

Waldi, who grew up in Germany during Hitler's regime, was an innocent member of Hitler Youth. The leaders encouraged children to tell whether anyone in their family opposed Hitler. Waldi shuddered to think how close she came to telling them that her parents hated Hitler. Had she done so, they would have been exterminated. Harley was a UT professor of population studies. A quiet man, he was no match for the voluble Waldi.

The site was a welcome challenge for Tom. Heavily wooded, it sloped down to a creek where Karl and Daniel and the Browning boys liked to play. Tom designed a house perched on piers to avoid disturbing the land. Made of rough cedar siding, the house had many large windows looking into the forest and at the creek below.

Tom continued to win awards for his architectural design. He was commissioned to design Briarcliff Golf and Yacht Club for a resort community on Lake Travis. For this project he won another Austin Chapter AIA award for excellence in design. *The Texas Architect* magazine said this:

"The architects chose to accentuate a limestone ledge forming the northeast crest of Briarcliff's highest hill by stretching a picturesque cluster of wooden buildings along its edge. Interiors surprise visitors with constant changes in volume and floor levels, rich colors and textures, and dramatic views of pools, the hills, and Lake Travis."

BRIARCLIFF GOLF AND COUNTRY CLUB

LAKE TRAVIS   NEAR AUSTIN, TEXAS

T A N I G U C H I ,   S H E F E L M A N ,   V A C K A R
A . I . A .   A R C H I T E C T S
AUSTIN   TEXAS

Tom called the architectural style "Country Bauhaus." It was also inspired by the architecture of Sea Ranch, which has a similar setting high above a body of water. He designed the buildings to have shed roofs sloping down to the lake, following the lay of the land.

Tom's favorite structural engineer and dear friend, Clark Craig, worked with him on the design. Ishmael made a mural for the dining room out of scrap pieces of rough cedar from the construction, nailing them together into a row of miniature buildings. When Tom brought the boys on the job, they made their own small versions. How they loved to make things with their hands, just like their dad.

Daniel remembers one of those visits when Tom took the boys down to Cat Hollow, an inlet where rocky cliffs rise above the water. They were climbing around on the rocks, investigating the caves. Suddenly Daniel realized he had almost stepped on a water moccasin! A father and sons adventure that I heard about later.

After some ten years, Willie Nelson bought the Briarcliff lodge, condominiums, and golf course. He turned the lodge into his recording studio. Tom, Daniel, and I drove out to Briarcliff not so long ago as a surprise tour for Tom's birthday. We were warmly welcomed by one of Willie's associates.

"This building has soul," he told Tom.

Then came Tom's huge urban renewal project, the project of his dreams. The City of Austin decided to celebrate its 1976 bicentennial by developing a long-range plan for Lower Waller Creek from 10th Street to Town Lake, as it was called then. TSVM, with Tom as the partner in charge, teamed up with a Dallas urban landscape firm, Myrick-Newman-Dahlberg, along with Freese and Nichols, an engineering firm, and were awarded the project. Tom became the project coordinator not only of these firms but also with the City.

Instead of turning its back on the part of Waller Creek that runs through the east side of Congress Avenue, the City wanted to embrace it, and so did Tom and his team. He advocated mixed land use for the urban area, meaning both commercial and residential use of the creek's edge.

Waller Creek Development Plan, 1975

Since Austin has creeks in all four quadrants, the overall plan was to connect the four to Town Lake with hike and bike trails and thus to each other. The Shoal Creek path had already been partially finished, thanks to the donation of Russell Fish. His family lived on the west side of the creek on Windsor Road and kept a horse to ride along its banks. We were neighborhood friends.

One year Russell asked his wife Jeannette what she wanted for her birthday.

"Perhaps a sports car?" he suggested.

"No," she said, "I want a hike and bike path on Shoal Creek that everyone can use."

Not only did she get her wish, she maintained the path and watered plants and trees when needed as she rode up and down the path in Russell's golf cart, usually with one of her sons or a hired man. What a legacy she left the city as well as a place where our neighborhood children could play and explore.

The Waller Creek project began with Tom and team walking and photographing the creek from 10th Street down to Town Lake. It was a mess of garbage, erosion, crumbling retaining walls, and water pollution. The team visualized condominiums, restaurants, and businesses there instead. But to make it so, there needed to be flood control, which they estimated would cost $50,000 at the time. Unfortunately the City decided they could not afford it. Even so, a part of the plan was built, particularly in the area surrounding 6th Street. Ironically, a Waller Creek flood tunnel has now been constructed for $161 million, and it is flawed by shoddy work. Would it have been better built for $50,000 in 1976 with supervision by Tom's team? I think so.

13

Swimming

*I*t all started with an alligator, Joe Boling, and Mark Spitz.
Tom, an excellent swimmer both above and under water, taught
Karl and Daniel how to swim. Daniel described the process at Tom's
memorial service.

"He also taught me how to swim. Joe Boling had something to
do with it later. The technique was that Tom told me to pretend I was
an alligator in the shallow end of Deep Eddy Pool and walk on my
hands until I got to the deep part and I was swimming. That's how I
learned to swim, like an alligator learns to swim. And I think I taught
my kids the same way. Also, riding on his back like a turtle. Even
though I knew how to swim I would pretend that I didn't so I could
ride on his back."

Later lessons were at Northwest Pool with Joe Boling, who taught
Karl and Daniel to be competitive swimmers. That is where Karl first
dared to jump off the high diving board when he was eight, maybe nine
years old. I can still see him standing on the end of the board, trying to
muster the courage to jump.

No! Don't do it, I wanted to call to him, but held back. He needed to
prove himself to himself. And he did!

It was the 1972 Summer Olympics, when Mark Spitz won seven
gold medals for the United States that inspired them to be competitive
swimmers. We were at dinner, watching on our little black-and-white

Sony TV on the sideboard. The boys were thrilled when the final competition was over and Spitz had set a new record.

Seeing their enthusiasm, I asked, "Do you want to join the Austin Aquatic Club?"

They did. This choice would have lasting effects on our lives. It determined the college Karl and Daniel would attend, their athletic pursuits, the people in their lives, the girl Daniel would marry, a movie Karl would make, and even our opening our home to Kim Lacy, who was like a daughter and sister for two years.

I was not a swimming mom, but I was proud of their athletic endeavor and the manly physiques they developed as a result. Tom and I attended their meets, and I jumped up and down in the bleachers, cheering them on.

Karl began by working out with Coach Patterson in Gregory Gym Pool at UT and later joined the Austin High School swim team, coached by Keith Bell. He participated in meets in Austin and other cities in Texas, including Dallas and San Antonio.

In Karl's senior year, Dotson Smith coached high school students from all over Austin together because each school had only a handful of swimmers. Both Karl and Daniel thought he was a bit wacky, but he really cared about his team. I attended a regional swim meet in San Antonio and have a visual memory of standing in the bleachers and watching Karl swim the 100-yard freestyle. Dotson walked along the pool deck, following him, cheering him on. Karl was swimming the event like a sprint, and Dotson got so excited he began jumping up and down, urging him on. And then the sprint was over before the end and Karl ran out of steam. As he said later, "I was purely a sprinter — didn't have much endurance." The 50-yard freestyle was his best event.

Daniel, too, was coached by Dotson at Swim-A-Day for a time. Then he joined Longhorn Aquatics and worked out in the new UT Swim Center. He was not fond of his first coach there, who was stern and demanding and later found to be abusing eleven-year-olds. Gulp! I feel fortunate that Karl and Daniel never suffered such an experience. Daniel's favorite coach was Ed Reece.

"I did love Ed Reece," Daniel said. "He coached Longhorn Aquatics in the summer. Those were my favorite workouts." Daniel's best event was the backstroke.

Workout schedules were challenging. Karl and Daniel had to get up before dawn. I would hear them leave and wondered how they did it.

And now about the daughter swimming brought us, Kim Lacy. Along with other swimmers, she came to Austin to work out with the famous and later infamous coach at Longhorn Aquatics. Families in the swimming community took these out-of-town kids into their homes.

Kim also attended Austin High, and one day Daniel came home from school and said that Kim asked if she could come live with us.

"She's unhappy with the family she's living with now. The mother doesn't cook, and there's no wholesome food in the house."

"I don't know, Daniel. That's a big deal."

"You'd like her, Mom. Maybe she could come over for dinner some night," he suggested, "so you and Tom could get to know her."

Tom was willing so I said okay.

In a few days Daniel brought her over. A pretty, blonde, and athletic girl, she was modestly dressed, wearing flat Baby Jane shoes. The picture of innocence. Though pretty, she did not seem obsessed by her looks and she had a sense of humor. I liked her immediately.

After talking with Tom that night, we decided to invite her to come live with us. Karl was away at Kenyon but we did not want her to use his room and share a bath with Daniel. We set up Kim's room in Tom's former studio, down the hall from our bedroom, and we shared a bath. Don't ask me how — we just managed. Kim made it easier by keeping all her bath supplies in a kit in her room. Tom set up his drawing board in the recreation room in the Little House. He also constructed a freestanding closet for her. As for my writing, I had my old Dallas desk in our bedroom and worked there. Later Tom would remodel Kim's room for my studio.

I never saw those Baby Janes again! We all laughed about this later when Kim admitted she tried hard to look acceptable. And it worked. But she was so much more than acceptable. She appreciated the good food and scheduled meals and our loving family. I felt happy to be her mom for those two years. She gave me the opportunity to know what it was like to have a daughter, including some makeup tips.

Years later after we lost Tom, Kim wrote to me:

You and Tom have always inspired me with your love ... equal, respectful, tender ... Modeling this to me as an adolescent was a powerful seed of hope in what a relationship could be.

Daniel and Kim became like brother and sister. One night at dinner Kim told us about something that happened at school. A bully accosted her, and Kim told him to leave her alone or she would tell her brother Daniel to take care of him.

"Oh, thanks a lot, Kim," Daniel said, half joking, because this bully was a real brute and violent.

Fortunately nothing ever came of it but a big laugh.

14

Camping Trips

*W*e made two camping trips to the beach at Galveston, the first in 1963. We rented a pop-up camper and hauled it to Friendswood behind our Rambler station wagon. After staying a few days with the Hensleys, we drove on to Galveston and parked on the beach between the sand dunes and the upper reaches of the tide. We raised the camper top, extended the awning, and set up folding chairs. Early morning and late afternoons we walked along the beach, picked up seashells, and built sand castles.

Karl's Sandcastle

We liked this campout so much we did it again in 1966 with the same pop-up camper. It had four bunks with screens all around, and we had the beach mostly to ourselves.

At night we lay in our bunks and listened to the waves roll in. It was the best sleeping ever, except when Karl got sunburned and found out there was sand in his sleeping bag.

Galveston Beach Campout

During the heat of day we napped and sat in the shade of our awning, watching the seagulls swoop about and the waves crawl up the beach and back again.

The next year we camped on the beach in Port Aransas.

Three years later, in 1970, we started our backpacking and hiking trips. I had decided not to encourage Karl and Daniel to join the Boy Scouts, and they showed no interest. Bill Wilson did not become a Scout either, but John Newman did. My thought was for our family to take camping trips instead. I prided myself in being able to keep up with Tom and the boys.

We borrowed a family-size tent from one of Tom's employees and set out for Enchanted Rock near Fredericksburg. There we set up our tent in the small campground, made a campfire, and cooked hot dogs, followed by s'mores.

Tom and Daniel Walk the Beach

The next morning we set out to climb the great pink granite dome that rises 425 feet out of the surrounding land. We carried lunch and canteens of water for a picnic on the top. Enchanted Rock is a long sloping climb, but some parts are steeper and toward the top quite barren, making the climb scary. Even though Daniel was only eight years old, he made it. We sat and ate our lunch on what seemed like the top of the world.

This was a trial run for our trip to Big Bend during the upcoming Easter holiday. Taking the same tent, we drove and drove until we arrived at Fort Davis, the highest town in Texas at 5,050 feet. I had made reservations at the Indian Lodge, a charming old hotel built in the 1930s in the white adobe style and set in the scrubby hills outside the town. I could have stayed there the whole time. The next morning we explored the historic Fort, built for protection from Comanches, Kiowas, and Apaches. That night we drove a few miles to McDonald Observatory and looked at the sky.

The most dramatic sky event happened while we were camped in the Chisos Basin in Big Bend at an elevation of 5,400 feet. Being there is like landing on another planet, so brutal and stark are the mountains. Our tent faced The Window, a V-shaped opening in the surrounding rocky cliffs, revealing the valley far below. In the dark of night a comet named Tago-Sato-Kosaka streaked across that opening as we watched. What an exciting treat for all four of us. I felt proud that Tom and I had brought the boys here.

Years later in 2017, Karl, Ellen, Daniel, Jane, and I drove to Big Bend for my birthday. It was a second trip for the Shefelmans, sadly without Tom, and a first for Ellen and Jane. Just before leaving Austin we had a ceremony of spreading Tom's ashes in a garden of wildflowers and a pecan tree near the Opossum Temple.

During the summer of 1970 we set out for Arizona to see the Grand Canyon, Mesa Verde, and the Rocky Mountains. I wanted Karl and Daniel to experience more of the United States. Later we would encourage them to see the world, as Tom and I had done, to know and respect other cultures. Thus the world map beside our dining table.

Karl at Grand Canyon

We camped on the South Rim of the Grand Canyon. The size and depth of the canyon is breathtaking. I could not sleep that night for worrying about our trip on mules that would take us halfway down the canyon the next morning. What if the mules made a misstep and sent us tumbling to the bottom? Those mules knew what they were doing, though, and no such thing happened. Daniel's mule was named Mister Ed.

From there we drove on to Mesa Verde in the Four Corners region of Colorado and set up our tent.

Mesa Verde

Beginning in the 12th Century the Pueblo Indians built stone cities with multi-storied buildings there, sheltered by overhangs in the cliffs. We visited the largest of these cliff cities, Cliff Palace, peeked into doorways, and climbed down a ladder into one of the round sunken kivas, which were used for religious rituals and ceremonies. Near the central firepit was a small hole called a *sipapu* where the Pueblo Indians believed their ancestors could return to this world. Oh, if only I had a *sipapu* for Tom, Mother, Daddy, and Mama, my maternal grandmother.

Next we traveled to Florida River, then on to Taylor River to camp and fish.

Karl loved fishing and making fires while Daniel loved making fires and cooking. Sometimes he scrambled a dozen eggs for our breakfast, and we consumed all of them! As soon as we arrived at a river or lake, Karl got out his fishing kit, which had a collapsible rod. He was a good, patient fisherman.

At Taylor River he helped Daniel pull in a big trout and caught it in a fishing bag. Then Tom oversaw their cleaning of the fish with his hunting knife. Karl looked awed by the job, Daniel looked repulsed, and Tom looked amused and proud of his sons. And I was proud of their love of camping out in nature.

Fishing at Taylor River

Cleaning Fish

On to Pikes Peak, where we camped at an isolated place near the base. That night Daniel woke up coughing. I, the family worrier, could not sleep. Did he have pneumonia? We had no way to contact anyone, other than get in the car and drive back to Colorado Springs. Fortunately my fears were unfounded, and he was fine the next morning. We drove to the summit at 14,115 elevation. Daniel was only eight years old and not ready to climb a fourteener. We would do that later on Mt. Rainier.

During the summer of 1971 we took a different kind of trip to the northeast coast and stayed in youth hostels. With backpacks and nylon sleeping sacks, we flew to Washington D.C. My idea was to educate Karl and Daniel, give them an adventure, and save money. The trip did all of the above, even though there were objections to some of the hostels along the way.

We landed at the then futuristic Dulles Airport, and took a bus into the city to the Hilton Hotel, which was near our hostel. Our backpacks felt heavy and conspicuous on our walk from there to 16th and P Streets, and I began to wonder if I had made the right decision.

It was a strangely mixed neighborhood north of the White House, and did not feel entirely safe. Old townhouses, some restored and some needing repair, lined the streets. Among them were many foreign embassies. We were amused at the Russian embassy, an elegant Victorian, well guarded and kept. As Tom described it:

"Up on the roof was a wonder world of antennas, wires, cables, loops, scopes, probes, and other electronic things."

Our hostel was in one of the old, once elegant townhouses. The cost was $2.20 per night for adults, $1.10 for children, and we got what we paid for. We had a family room, which had metal bunk beds and no air conditioning. Tom wrote four pages of impressions of this hostel and our arrival:

1 August 1971 10:15 PM
The motherly and fatherly house parents seemed to give us

confidence. Also, my immediate acquaintance with Japanese, Indian, and Thai people made us begin to feel at ease. Note that Karl and Daniel seemed considerably more pragmatic about travel experience so far today than we were. For them it may simply be novel.

The weather was hot and humid so our nylon sleeping bags on bare mattresses were miserable. Here are Tom's comments about a family discussion as we lay in our metal beds that night.

Windows must remain open & it rains in — but it's an old urban sensation to hear rain splattering in a courtyard below.
"It's so hot in here — in these dumb sheets." (Daniel)
"It's not exactly like staying in Disneyland Hotel." (Karl)
"Do you like our strange journey?" (Mom)

Nevertheless, we were up early the next morning, and I fixed breakfast in the communal kitchen, which was empty.

Of all the sights — the White House, the Capitol, the Smithsonian, and Mt. Vernon — the most emotional experience was the Lincoln Memorial. It was for me, at least, and I suspect for the boys as well. The building is in the style of an open Doric temple. The giant statue of Lincoln, arms resting on the throne-like chair as he looks down solemnly upon the tiny people at the base, makes one feel the man's enormous effect on our country.

Afterward, Karl and Daniel enjoyed sliding down the wide marble banisters on the front steps. I think Abe would have enjoyed watching them.

From Washington we took Amtrak to Philadelphia where we stayed at Chamounix, a restored mansion turned into a hostel, situated high above the Schuylkill River. The place was immaculate, so much so that after I fixed breakfast the next morning in the large, modern kitchen, washed the dishes, and put them away, the manager pointed out that I needed to dry the drops of water left in the sink. Though I never did any such thing at home, I complied.

The manager lived in the hostel with her husband and a St. Bernard named Thor. He terrified me, especially with a name like that. Dogs seem to smell my fear and bark at me. But Thor and Daniel took a liking to each other. If Thor stood on his hind legs like Daniel, he would be the taller of the two, with a larger head and mouth.

Next we took the train to New York. Little did I imagine that Karl and Daniel would one day live and work there. To travel around the city we used the subway. To get to our hostel in Queens, we had to go down many steps to the lowest level on a sweltering day.

"I feel like I'm going down into hell," Daniel said.

I agreed and lived in fear of being separated from them every time we boarded or exited the train.

Our hostel was in a dormitory on the NYU campus. All four of us slept crosswise on a double bed. What was I thinking?

Manhattan was an adventure, everything from a carriage ride in Central Park, a visit to FAO Schwarz on Fifth Avenue, the Statue of Liberty, which made a BIG impression on both boys, a view from the top of the Empire State building, then the highest in the city, to the Chrysler Building with its unique steeple, red granite walls, ceiling mural of workers, and Egyptian elevator doors. The most beautiful building in the world, I think.

Then on to Boston by train. Probably Boston was the best city experience of all, despite the hostel being in the basement of a church in Dorchester, where hanging sheets separated the men's and women's sleeping areas.

Before our trip I had read *Johnny Tremain* to Karl and Daniel. Thus, when we followed the red bricks on the Freedom Trail that took us to many sites in the book, they were thrilled to walk on cobblestone streets and find Paul Revere's real house.

"Wow! I can't believe his house is still here," Karl called as he strode ahead. Yes, the small gray clapboard house still stands on its original site, no worse for the years.

Thor and Daniel

Of course, we had read *Make Way for Ducklings* long before, and one never forgets that story. So finding the pond and the swan boats on the Boston Common and riding in one was a thrill, rivaled only by the *USS Constitution*. Books make connections with real places.

From Boston we took the train to Hyannis and a ferry to Nantucket. This little island seemed far, far away from land, a world isolated from time and change. We rented bicycles and rode to our youth hostel, about three miles from town on the beach. My heart sang when I saw the two-story Victorian building with a lookout cupola and shingle siding painted slate blue. It was originally a lifesaving station built in 1873, hence the cupola and location near the beach.

Nantucket Beach

We parked our bicycles in the racks provided in back, where wash hung drying on a clothesline. Inside we found a comfortable living area and separate rooms for men and women upstairs — no hanging sheets. And there were wooden bunk beds instead of metal.

We explored the town with its preserved 19th century cobbled Main Street and sat on a bench to eat a snack of Ritz crackers and cheese. Later we played on the beach, taking turns burying each other's bodies in the sand. It was a welcome relief from all the sightseeing and a good rest for our hike in the White Mountains up to the top of Mt. Washington.

Nantucket Youth Hostel

We rented a car in Boston and drove through New Hampshire to a trailhead for the part of the Appalachian Trail that ascends Mt. Washington, the most prominent peak east of the Mississippi at 6,288 feet altitude. Only now, after researching the strenuous climb and dangerous, changing weather and winds possible up to 200+mph, do I marvel that we did it, especially since Daniel was only nine years old.

Mt. Washington Climb

Carrying our heavy backpacks, we climbed the steep, rocky trail up past the tree line, through intermittent fog. We took rests along the way and stopped to drink from mountain streams. Just when we thought we could go no farther, we sighted the Lakes of the Clouds Hut and the two blue lakes nearby, all above the clouds. The hut was actually a rambling residence perched on the mountainside. There we had a hearty meal and comfortable bunks for the night. This place was better than the top where there were more people and commerce.

Lake of the Clouds

Thus ended our second ascent of a mountain, the first being Enchanted Rock, but it would not be our last. The next summer of 1972 we headed to Aspen, Colorado, where Tom was to attend a design conference. We turned it into another camping trip. There was also a music festival going on.

We set up camp ten miles outside Aspen at a lake reflecting the Maroon Bells, twin 14,000-foot mountains of red shale shaped like bells. The lake was ice cold, and yet Karl braved the waters, briefly submerging himself and then dashing out. To Karl's delight, the fishing was good. He could spend hours patiently waiting for one of the trout to take his hook. And they did. Then Daniel's delight was frying the fish for dinner.

One of the places Karl fished was on the other side of the lake from our campsite. To reach it, he had to cross Maroon Creek on a large fallen tree while the water roared past below. I shudder to think what could have happened. He was fourteen and a strong swimmer but could he have held onto the bank if he fell?

Tom was always there when either boy walked the log, and I felt confident he could save them. But one time Daniel disappeared from our campsite without telling us where he was going. When Tom and I realized he was gone, we ran to the log.

"Daniel! Daniel, where are you?" we called frantically.

No answer, at least none that we could hear above the roar of water spilling over the rocks. I had a vision of him being washed downstream, hitting rocks, screaming for help. But he was nowhere to be seen. Tom and I walked the log to the other side and hurried to Karl's favorite fishing spot.

There was Daniel, watching him fish.

I was so relieved that I hugged him close. "Don't ever leave our campsite again without telling us where you're going."

Tom nodded. "Yes, Daniel, only with me watching you. Okay?"

Daniel agreed but did not seem overly impressed.

Boys! Well, I wanted us to have an adventure, and we were.

Karl Walking the Log

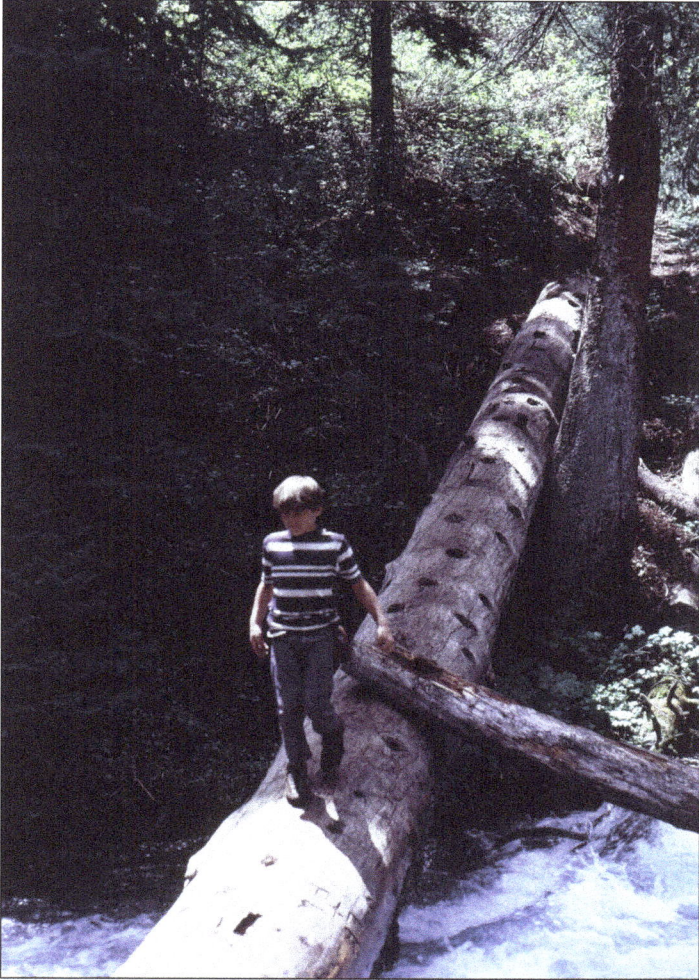

Daniel Walking the Log

While Tom attended programs at the design conference, Karl, Daniel, and I explored Aspen. I remember going into the historic Hotel Jerome. The sky-lighted lobby with a giant painting of the founder, Jerome Wheeler, over the fireplace, made me long to lounge on the sofa and stay there for the night. Alas, there is a price to pay for saving money and having adventures. It is called comfort.

Instead, I led the way into a record shop in the hotel. The room was filled with tropical plants and the music of minimalist composer, Terry Riley. I was enchanted, bought one of his albums, *A Rainbow in Curved Air,* and felt like a hippie girl. I think the boys liked it, too, because we played it often back home.

As for the music festival, we all attended a concert in a giant, octagonal tent designed by Eero Saarinen in 1949. The program featured the original piano version of "Pictures at an Exhibition" by Modest Mussorgsky. It was a memorable experience, both the tent architecture and the music.

Just as Daddy had helped me love Mozart and Beethoven by playing their music, I wanted Karl and Daniel to love classical music. At home they had a record player on a rolling table so that they could share it, and I made sure that the record holder below had classical music as well as Pete Seeger and the Weavers, and eventually the Beatles. Once a teacher, always a teacher, especially for our sons.

When the design conference was over, we set out on a four-day backpacking trip through the mountains on a loop trail from Maroon Lake. By this time we were acclimated to the 9,580 foot altitude at our campsite.

We hiked through flowering mountain meadows, past Aspen forests to Crater Lake, where we stopped for a snack. Then onward and upward. Once, Daniel lagged behind and Karl ran ahead.

"Daniel, beavers!" he called out, which got Daniel moving. We found Karl at a small lake and marveled at the perfectly shaped mound of a lodge that the beavers had built in the middle. The beavers must have been sleeping in their cozy lodge since they are nocturnal creatures.

From there the path became more difficult as we hiked above the tree line and over Willow Pass at 12,580 feet. At night we slept in our backpacking tent, warm in down-filled sleeping bags. We saw no black bears at our campsites but they were probably not attracted to our dried food supply or Tang, our orange-flavored powder for mixing with water. Who could forget Tang! I never will nor will I ever drink it again.

By day we hiked, rested and snacked, crossed precarious rocky slopes, marveled at the mountain views and crystal clear lakes until we descended again to a forest trail and finally Maroon Lake and our trusty Rambler station wagon.

This experience readied us for the ascent of Mount Rainier, but not quite.

15

Ascent of Mount Rainier

On a clear day Mount Rainier is visible from Seattle, rising above the Cascades in the distance. Although Tom hiked in the Cascades when he was a boy, he never climbed Rainier. Madolene probably would not allow him to do so. But I wanted our family to have adventures.

In planning a summer trip for 1974, I read a National Geographic book called *Vacationland U.S.A.* One of the vacations was a guided climb of Mount Rainier. We all got excited about it, and Tom decided we could follow the climb with sailing in the Puget Sound and then have a visit with Granddad. So I began making arrangements because that was always my role in the family.

Karl was fifteen years old and Daniel only eleven. According to the guide service, Rainier Mountaineering Incorporated, the youngest person ever to make the climb was an eight-year-old boy. After all our mountain climbing experience, I felt Daniel could do it. Little did I realize the difficulty of the climb, even though I knew we would need crampons and ice axes. The main concern about climbing Mount Rainier is the possibility of rapid weather change, and I had faith that R.M.I. would not take us up unless reports were favorable. After all, famed mountaineer Lou Whittaker ran the service, and it had an excellent reputation.

After a year of planning, we boarded a flight to Seattle with backpacks and luggage. Granddad met us at the airport and drove us to Paradise Inn, a rustic lodge in the style of national park architecture that some call parkitecture. The two-story lobby or Great Room has posts, exposed beams, and rafters made of cedar logs, all well lit by dormer windows. A massive grandfather clock made by a German craftsman stands sentinel beside the stone fireplace. With handcrafted furniture and a wood fire burning, the Great Room seemed both cozy and grand, a step back in time. We had two modest rooms with a bath down the hall, which was quite common when the inn was built. A simpler, less luxurious way of life that we hostel travelers were accustomed to.

Before dark that first evening Tom and I took a little stroll on a nearby path, and I began to get slightly short of breath. Could I do this? We were at 5,400 feet altitude. There were still 9,000 feet to go! I looked up at Rainier's peak that loomed above Paradise Inn like a mother goddess inviting her children to climb on her snowy flanks. Yes, I could.

In the morning, after renting boots, crampons, and ice axes, we attended climbing school with guides who would take us up the mountain the next day. The lessons would determine who could make the climb and who could not. Harold, Tom, and I had decided that if Daniel did not pass the test, he would stay with his granddad. The first lesson was how to self-arrest. We took turns climbing a practice slope, knowing that at some point our guides would jerk on the rope to pull us down. Our job was to self-arrest with ice axes. I began to get scared and hung back in line. If Tom and Karl were worried, they did not show it.

Daniel remembers that he was determined to go to the top of Rainier with us and not stay with Granddad. His will enabled him to stop himself when Greg, his guide, jerked the rope. He not only passed the test but also gave me courage.

When my turn came, I climbed, using the kick-step method to make a platform for my boot as the guides taught us. Suddenly I felt jerked down and dug in with my ice axe. It worked!

Probably because of my fear, I won the prize for self-arrest, according to my guide Joe. But I won no prize for putting on my crampons, which had loosened in the slide.

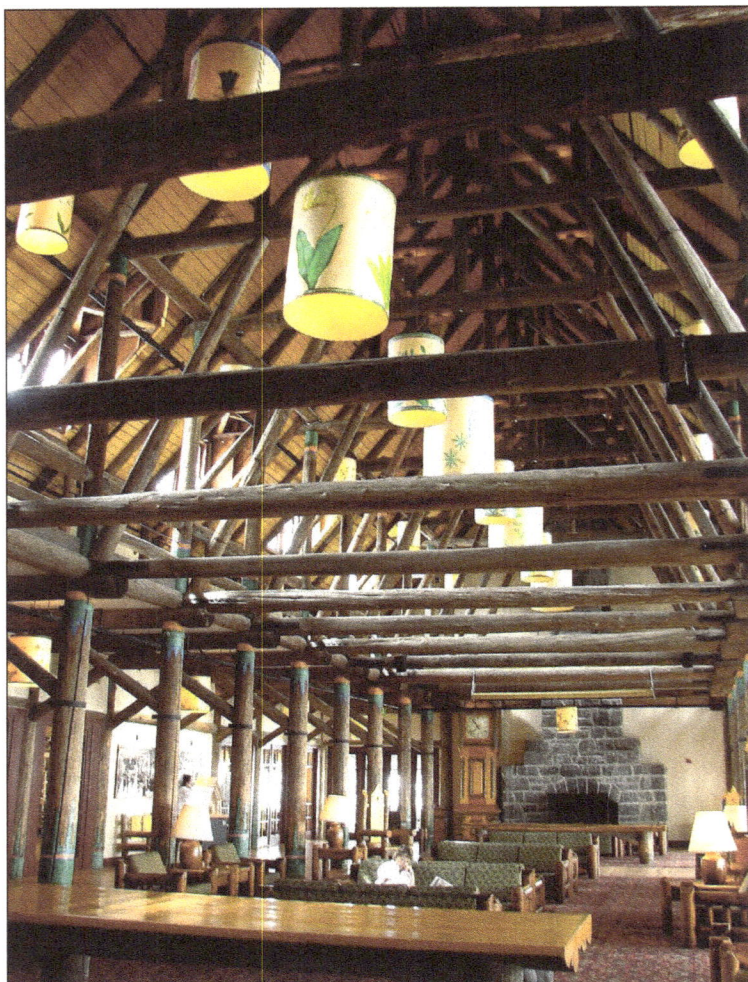

Paradise Inn

"Put them on tight," Joe said. "Tomorrow I don't want to stop anywhere on the mountain to adjust crampons."

That night after dinner we climbers and our guides gathered in the Guide House beside the trailhead to talk about the next day and why each of us wanted to climb Rainier.

"I grew up in Rainier's shadow and always dreamed of climbing it," Tom said.

I don't remember what the boys said. Maybe, "My mom made me do it." I said something stupid like, "To prove you're never too old." (I was only forty-four.)

Early the next morning we shouldered our backpacks and began our climb to Camp Muir, the base camp at 10,188 feet.

We followed the trail through meadows of wildflowers, past rock outcroppings where darting chipmunks stopped to watch us, along a mountain stream, past a waterfall and snow patches, and finally to snowfields above the tree line. The trail was steep in places but we were rewarded with views of Mount Adams and Mount St. Helens before it blew off its top.

At every rest stop I checked on the boys, who seemed to be doing fine. On one of our stops I looked above us and saw a tall bank of snow.

"That's called a serac," Joe told us. "It's the leading edge of a glacier."

That alarmed me. "Could it come loose and fall on us?"

"Probably not or we wouldn't be sitting here," Joe said.

Probably bothered me and I felt relieved when we moved on.

When we reached the Muir snowfield, we stopped to rest, strapped on our crampons, and proceeded. It seemed we would never get to Camp Muir. Finally, a couple of small buildings on a rocky plateau came into view in the distance.

Once there, R.M.I. provided dinner, which we ate sitting on rocks outside as we watched the sun set behind distant mountains. After using the pit toilet, we spread our sleeping bags on the wooden bunks in the public shelter. Our guides stayed in a rock shelter designed by a Seattle architect and built in 1917.

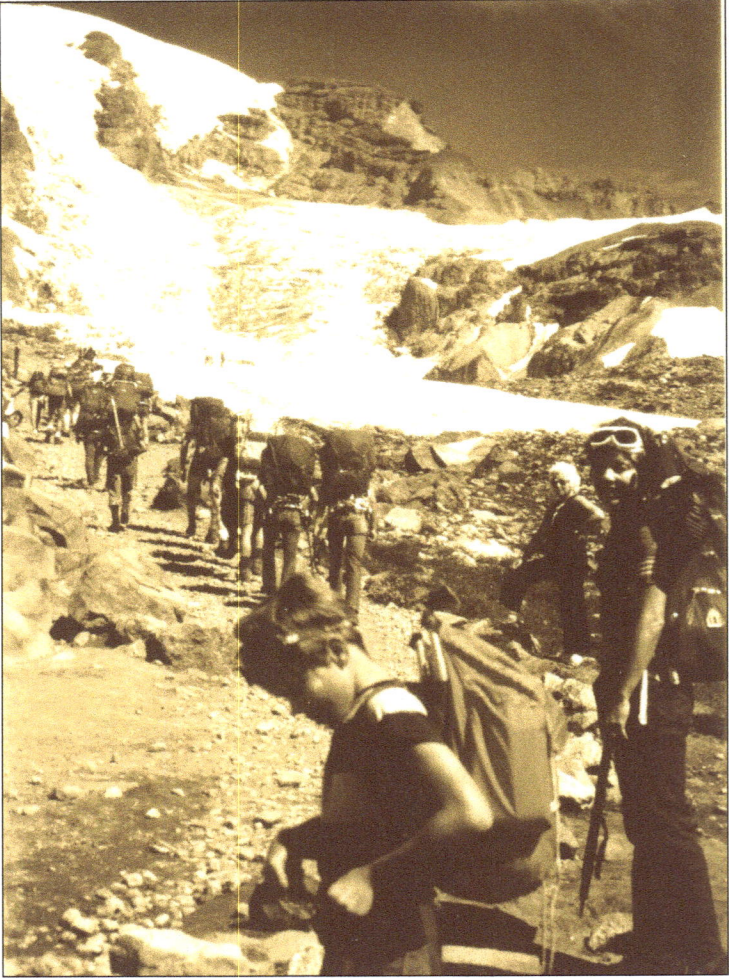

Mt. Rainier Start

I worried whether Karl and Daniel could sleep because one of the climbers snored. But sleep or not, the guides got us up at midnight in order to make the summit and down again before the noontime sun caused the snow to avalanche.

For breakfast we had a bowl of oatmeal, which Karl promptly threw up.

"Not uncommon," said Luke, his guide. "He'll be fine and we have snacks for the climb."

After everyone made a trip to the pit toilet, we lined up in the dark, put on our headlamps, crampons, and roped up — four teams of five people with a guide in the lead of each. The Shefelmans were put on separate teams so that we would not worry about each other, which only made me worry more. Still, we had excellent guides, some who had climbed in the Himalayas.

My team was to lead. It was comforting to see that both boys stood next in line behind their guides. Before Joe gave the signal to start, he took a pee, facing away from us. Since I was next behind him, I saw the stream hit the snow. That took confidence. He was definitely in charge.

At 1:30 a.m. he called, "Let's go!"

We crossed crevasses, some hundreds of feet deep and wide enough to require a bridge made of a ladder with wooden planks across it. Even with ropes connecting us and professionals ready to use their ice axes, it felt scary. Step by step and breath by breath we climbed in the night by the light of our headlamps, using the breathing technique the guides taught us — a long, deep inhale through the nose and a fast whooshing exhale through the mouth. In the distance we heard the thunder of an avalanche that sounded like the mountain was collapsing.

"I never heard anything like that before," Joe said.

What are we doing here on this mountain in the dark? I wondered.

Daniel remembers thinking, *I might die!*

The only time I got a glimpse of Tom and the boys was when we stopped to rest and drink water. I felt confident that Tom and Karl would make it but worried about Daniel. Still, he was first in line behind Greg, his guide, so I knew he was in good hands.

The air became thinner and we took rests as needed, sometimes on a rocky ridge that mountaineers call a cleaver because it separates two glaciers. It is also a good place to stop and rest.

"Where's the next cleavage?" Karl asked Luke.

The guides had a good laugh, and from then on cleaver was cleavage. Karl looked chagrined, but he was not far from right. Both words have the same root and mean a division, whether it be glaciers or breasts.

At last, dawn came and as the sun rose over a curved, glowing horizon, Joe called a rest halt. Scattered clouds drifted by below us, and we could see Mount Adams, Mount Baker, and Mount St. Helens peeking above them.

Then up and up, along Disappointment Cleaver, so named because of the climbers who had to turn back for various reasons, including high winds. But we were determined not to be disappointed.

We climbed through the snow, making kick steps. *Don't look up and don't look down, just look at the next step,* I told myself.

At last Joe reached the top and I was close behind. I unhooked myself and sat waiting. I could not rejoice until the Shefelmen made it.

Next, Greg appeared above the edge, holding the rope with Daniel struggling up the last few steps, bent under the effort and the weight of his backpack. Greg unfastened him and I helped remove his pack and sat beside him as he slumped on the snow.

"What a brave and strong boy you are," I said hugging him.

Then came Karl's team and Tom's. We had made it. We were 14,411 feet above sea level!

"I don't feel good," Daniel said. "I feel like throwing up."

I turned to Greg. "We have to go down, *now*," I told him.

Greg shook his head. "No, he'll be okay. He just needs to relax and breathe."

Daniel at the Summit

Karl at the Summit

Karl felt a little sick, too. When someone offered him a can of sardines, he just shook his head. Nor did he want to hike with Tom and some other climbers around the rim of the crater to the far side, which was the highest point and where there was a book to sign. So Tom signed for all of us. My problem was that I needed to have a BM, so I went behind a rock and left my sign, perhaps still frozen on the summit.

As we sat, recovering our strength and breath, a jet headed for SeaTac airport flew in below us. How amazing to look down on an airplane full of people! The only disappointment was that we could not see Seattle because of clouds, but we could see peaks of the Cascade Range to the south.

After a lengthy rest and some snacks as tolerated, we roped up and began our descent, which felt almost harder than our ascent, at least for me.

"I don't want to hear any knee complaints," Joe said, so I kept them to myself. As we descended below Camp Muir and got off the ropes, Tom, Karl, Daniel, and others delighted in glissading down snowfields. But not I or another woman. We lagged behind with a couple of assistants, a girl and her boyfriend who did not seem to mind following us in a leisurely descent. We were the last ones down.

The Shefelmen, including Harold, were waiting for me in the Great Room. After showers in the bathroom down the hall, Harold treated us to a celebration dinner. Our guides sat at a table nearby.

"Are you young men in college?" Harold asked them in his formal manner, stretching his chin upward.

"Yes, sir; no ,sir," came their uninterested replies. End of conversation.

So, what do the Shefelmans do next after climbing Mount Rainier? Charter a 28-foot sailboat and cruise in the San Juan Islands for a week.

16

Sailing and the San Juan Islands

*T*om started sailing when he was a boy at Camp Westward Ho in the San Juan Islands. The campers made trips across the Strait of Juan de Fuca and up to Victoria. Then at Camp Coeur d'Alene in Idaho he not only sailed in the lake but also built boats in the crafts workshop. Making things, sailing, and drawing were in his blood.

When I first met Tom he was rebuilding a Snipe, a 14-foot centerboard boat that he had rescued from a shallow place at Greathouse Harbor on Lake Travis. He, Bill Carter, Eugene George, and other boat builders had a workshop on Red River Street in downtown Austin. Tom was in the process of covering the wooden hull with fiberglass.

During that summer, before Tom and I were married, my friend Jane Allman and I moved to Austin and rented an apartment next to the UT campus. She had a boyfriend here and I had Tom. I managed to get a job with the City of Austin Parks and Recreation Department teaching arts and crafts in east and south Austin parks, which is another story.

Briefly told, Tom let me use his Plymouth to drive to various parks. I had taught crafts like basket weaving and lanyards at Camp Fern near Marshall when I was a student at SMU. The park kids loved making stuff with their hands. Once the Pan American Recreation Center on the east side was locked down because of a gang war threat, but fortunately nothing came of it.

Back to Tom's boat workshop. I often joined the guys there and helped Tom sand the mahogany trim. For breaks one of them would buy a watermelon for us. Since the workshop was not air-conditioned, this was a real treat.

When Tom finished work on the Snipe, we took it out for a maiden voyage, launching from Greathouse Harbor on a Monday after work. Why we did so on a weekday remains a mystery.

It was my first sail since Pat Mosher, a college friend, took me out on White Rock Lake for a July 4th celebration. That sail was uneventful, but not this one!

The wind was brisk, and we wasted no time getting out in the lake. Tom manned the tiller and mainsail while I womaned the jib. We flew up the lake on a run, past Starnes Island. As darkness fell we headed back for our harbor, tacking all the way, both of us leaning out on the windward side to keep the boat from capsizing.

Suddenly there was a loud crack, and the mast fell to one side, sail and all dragging in the water.

"What happened?" I yelled.

"The mast broke, but we'll be okay," Tom said as he leaped up and began pulling the mast onto the deck and gathering the sail. "Let the jib fly."

We slowed and began to drift while the jib flapped.

As Tom struggled to get the sail out of the water and onto the boat, he said, "Get the flashlight, Janice, and send an SOS. You know, three short, three long, three short flashes."

I didn't know but I did it. The problem was that there were no other boats on the lake, and in 1954 few people lived on the shores.

When Tom got the mast and mainsail secured, he rowed us close to shore and pulled up the centerboard, a task demanding tremendous strength. We pulled the Snipe onto land, tied her to a boulder, and hiked back to the Plymouth. Turned out that the mast broke because one of the shrouds sheered, allowing the strong wind to blow the mast over.

The next day Tom took the trailer, loaded the Snipe, and brought it back to town. This happened shortly before our wedding so he did not have time to repair the mast. A sailor friend, Don Marsh, offered to repair the mast and sail the Snipe while we were gone. Clark Craig offered his garage and helped with the repair. Bless them. That Snipe was the only large item that we did not sell before leaving, and it became the boat that Karl and Daniel first knew, if not loved.

A Snipe is really a two-person boat, not meant for a family. Once when we took the boys sailing, we capsized, dumping us all into the lake. We all wore life jackets but still it was scary.

"I don't like this. I'm not going sailing anymore," said Daniel, who was only six years old.

So we sold the Snipe and bought a 22-foot sailboat, which had a fin keel, making it more stable and giving us a bigger cockpit. It also had a small cabin. Daniel changed his mind about sailing and named her *Brave Sails,* perhaps for his own bravery.

Sailing Party

The drive out to Lake Travis was long and winding, which sometimes made the boys carsick, especially Daniel. We had numbers for how

sick: 1) Starting to feel sick, 2) Prepare to pull over, 3) Stop the car —
I'm going to throw up.

Another problem was that Karl and Daniel loved to watch *Wild Kingdom* on Sunday nights. They became impatient with taking down and folding the sails and the long drive home. So we made an effort to come in earlier.

Gradually sailing became a Shefelman family trait. For one of Karl's birthdays we had a Split Rock sailing party. Tom and the boys made little wooden boats with sails as favors for each child, and we went downbelowthecliff and sailed them on the pond.

Tom was a charter member of the Austin Sailing Club. When they purchased property up the lake a little way and built docks and a lodge, we moved our boat there. We hosted a few birthday parties at the club, and Tom took the boys and their friends out for a sail. I stayed on land and set up snacks and birthday cake.

Though I had crewed for Tom in races on Lake Travis, I didn't care much for it, maybe because we never won. Eventually we decided on sailing and camping, sold *Brave Sails* and bought a Pearson Electra, which had a bigger cabin and bunks. We named it *Dulcinea*, our ladylove, and took her out for camping trips.

This experience gave us the confidence to arrange a cruise in the San Juan Islands after climbing Mount Rainier. We chartered a 28-foot yacht named *Duchess* and picked her up from the owner at his dock on Whidbey Island. She was equipped with charts, maps, compass, tide tables, and life jackets. After loading our groceries and duffel bags, we hoisted the sails and set out.

The gateway to the San Juans was through Deception Pass between Whidbey and Fidalgo Islands. Tom had experienced sailing through this narrow pass and into the Strait of Juan de Fuca. He knew the treachery of the rapid current at ebb and flow, up to eight knots with turbulent eddies and rips. So we timed ourselves to sail through during slack tide.

What a glorious gateway to our sailing adventure. We passed between steep cliffs on either side and under the airy arched bridge high above, built of steel in 1935. And there we were in the vast Strait of Juan de Fuca with Lopez Island ahead in the distance.

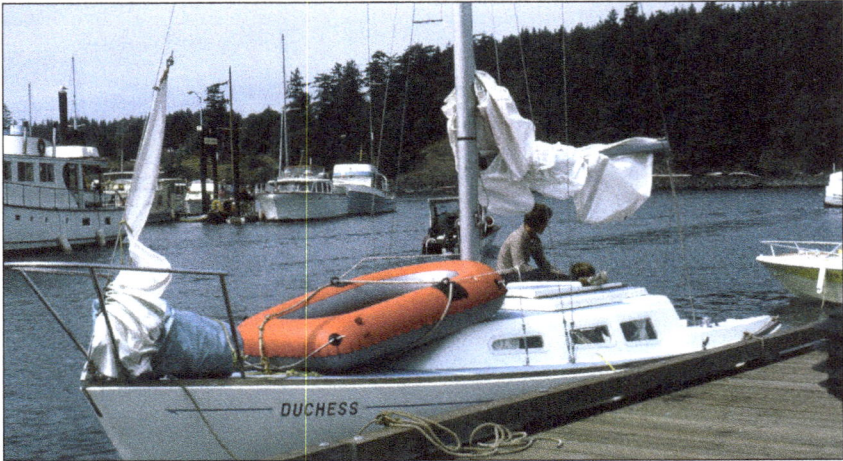

Tom on the Duchess

Tom had taken a course in coastal navigation and successfully guided us to Friday Harbor on San Juan Island by late afternoon. We docked and enjoyed stretching our legs as we walked up the hill on Spring Street, which is lined with charming little shops, coffee houses, and restaurants.

Fisherman Karl

We stayed there for a couple of days. Tom sketched and took photos. Karl fished from the dock and once caught a long string of seaweed. Daniel combed the beach for oysters, and I cooked their catch, except for the seaweed. Meanwhile the ferries came and went several times a day, announcing arrival and departure with three horn blasts, one long and two short.

Daniel Digs for Oysters

From there we sailed along the northern coast of San Juan Island to Roche Harbor and docked below the historic Hotel de Haro. Built in 1886, it is a three-story white frame structure with balconies across the second and third stories, facing the harbor and overlooking a garden. We decided to dine and stay the night there. Again, the bath was down the hall and we took it over.

The next day we hiked around the village. Near the hotel is a small white chapel, Our Lady of Good Voyage. Tom made a felt marker drawing of it from our dock at night under a full moon.

Then on to Deer Harbor on Orcas Island for one night. My most vivid memory of this harbor is the wild blackberries growing on bushes along the path up to the village, waiting for us to pick and eat.

Jones Island, our next stop, is a Washington State Park and un-inhabited. We tied up to a buoy and took our rubber dinghy to the shoreline. Tame deer welcomed us or the food we might have. All we had were bananas. We ate the bananas and fed the peels to the deer, which they seemed to like. Then we hiked through the forest to the opposite shore where there was another cove with a large sailing yacht tied up. Our two boats were the only ones at the island.

In the morning we awoke to a dense fog that completely closed us in. Tom knew about such fogs in this part of the world, his world.

"It'll lift soon," he assured us. And it did, soon but slowly.

Our final stop was in one of the northernmost of the San Juans, Sucia Islands, also a state park. Rocky shores surround the main island. We moored in Echo Bay and took our dinghy to the great curving shoreline. There we combed the beach, climbed on the rocks, and searched for fossils.

Karl remembers taking the dinghy out alone in the bay to fish. He caught a spiny rockfish and feared it might puncture the dinghy. But being the fisherman he is, he managed to get it off the hook and toss it back without puncturing his hands or the dinghy. He did catch a flounder and brought it to our boat for dinner. Daniel did not have the will or patience for fishing. He would rather cook a fish than catch one.

By this time the close quarters of the *Duchess* began to wear on us. One night a shouting match between Tom and Karl erupted as we were dining. Karl was a teenager and needed some space. Peace was restored the next day when Tom let Karl skipper as we headed home through the Strait of Georgia in the cold wind. We donned our yellow rain gear and were grateful when we made it back through Deception Pass into protected waters.

Granddad met us at the owner's home and whisked us to a Seattle hotel. After we showered and dressed, he treated us to dinner in a restaurant where he was well known, so we had some welcome pampering.

Back in Austin we continued to sail, but Lake Travis seemed small by comparison. My best memories are the night sails under a full moon with

Karl and Daniel, a friend or two, and classical music from KMFA playing on our trusty little radio. It felt like floating in another world, free of any ties to Earth, among the stars. One such night, an adolescent Daniel stood beside the mast, looking up at the purple sky. He pointed and said, "Look, there's Orion!" His voice broke for the first time on the word Orion.

Skipper Karl

Another night when Tom and I were out alone on the lake with no other boats around, I remember hearing Beethoven's "Egmont Overture" by moonlight. An unforgettable moment, never to happen again.

Even though none of our family was as enthusiastic about sailing as Tom, especially raising and lowering and folding the sails, Karl and Daniel became expert sailors and raced with him. Sometimes they disagreed about who was skipper, especially Daniel, who thought he knew better.

By the time each of the boys reached high school and could drive, they occasionally went sailing on their own with friends. Daniel took a group of boys, John Newman, Reed Stephenson, Gabe Thornhill, and Marc Shivers on a camping trip up Lake Travis. From all reports it was a blast.

Once when Karl took a girl sailing on a date, she complained about mosquitoes. "You just have to ignore it," he replied, which did not win points with her.

Back at home Karl told me the story and complained, "Mom, you can't get any girls with a sailboat. It takes a motorboat and water skis."

"Maybe not, but you could get the *right* girl," I said. "Just don't ignore her feelings about mosquito bites."

17

Friday Mountain Camp

*W*hen Karl and Daniel came of age, we sent them to spend two
weeks at Friday Mountain Boys Camp every summer. The mostly
male environment seemed a good change from female teachers and an
ever-present mom. Both of our boys loved the place and the people and
went on to become counselors. The camp was owned and run by Captain
Kidd, his wife, Von, and son Walter.

The land was originally the site of the Johnson Institute, a school
that opened in 1853 in a two-story limestone building with thick walls
and seven fireplaces. The limestone was quarried on the property. Texas
historian Walter Prescott Webb bought the property in 1942, restored
the building, and took care of the land. In 1946 he and his friend Rodney
Kidd decided to open a camp there. Eventually Webb sold the property
to the Captain, knowing he would preserve it. And he did.

Friday Mountain Camp had history and character. Much of the
character came from the Captain. He was the heart of the camp. But the
heart stopped and the camp closed in 1984. Since then a Hindu religious
group bought the property. Though they did not tear down the historic
limestone building, they built a multi-million dollar temple nearby with
pink Chinese granite and gold leaf. An unsettling contrast.

Shortly afterward, Tom, Karl, and I drove out to see the once
Friday Mountain Camp, and I rather wish we never had. Entering the
incongruous temple, we got permission to roam around the grounds

and remember the camp that once was. The various cabins were still standing but in disrepair. As we stepped inside the Stallions cabin, Karl said, "Well, this is another closed door on my past."

But we have vivid memories of the camp, the old limestone building that served as dining room and kitchen with staff rooms upstairs, Friday Mountain rising above the surroundings, Bear Creek, Windy Cove swimming hole, where boys swung out from a rocky ledge and dropped into the cool, clear water. Such simple pleasures.

My memories of the camp are of parents visiting days, one after the first week and another at the end of the second. Tom and I and other parents followed our boys to their various activities, horseback riding, rifle range, archery, swimming, and crafts. At noon there was a buffet lunch served under the live oaks around the old stone building. Afterward, Captain Kidd told stories about the camp in his charming country boy way.

He was a good storyteller. On Sundays he led the boys to a spot on Bear Creek that was like an amphitheater for a church service. It was a serene place in nature with only the sounds of flowing water and birdsong. The boys sat on logs as Captain told long moral stories, and wife Von led the boys in singing "The Old Rugged Cross" and "Bringing in the Sheaves," among others. Meanwhile Jewish boys were bused to a nearby temple. At the time, Karl did not know what being Jewish meant, but he was impressed that they were taken to their own temple.

As for horseback riding, Karl remembers Mr. Gravell, the "crusty curmudgeon but very lovable" stable master. Daniel said, "His favorite thing to do was taze us with a cattle prod." Karl's favorite horse was a mare named Candy, just like Young Wolf and his Red Wind.

The handcrafts workshop counselor was Mr. Dorn, who Karl said was "a cranky perfectionist with no sense of humor." Still, Karl and Daniel had learned so much from Tom about making things that they excelled. Among other projects, Karl made a lamp using a cut log, which he sanded and varnished. It has lighted our home ever after. And Daniel made a leather wallet with a pressed design of a flower around Tom's name.

Karl Riding Candy

The rifle range and archery were favorite activities for both boys. They liked shooting weapons and the smell of gunpowder. One of the counselors had an elephant gun that made an impressive blast.

Daniel Second from Right

"Friday Mountain had a unique Texas Hill Country rustic quality to it you wouldn't find in, say, a camp up in Pennsylvania or New York

– very rugged, very hot," Karl said.

He had two favorite counselors. One was Leslie Flowers in the Colt's cabin, "a big muscular guy who played his guitar and sang to us at night." The other was Steve when Karl was a Stallion. "When it was time for us to take showers, Steve would yell, 'GET NAKED' so loud it could be heard all over camp."

Karl and Counselors

Sometimes the counselors told ghost stories at night, like the one about Otis, the mentally disturbed brother of the old Black cook, Wilson. Supposedly Otis lived in an abandoned bus on the edge of the property. People started seeing blood on his hands, and he explained that he had killed an animal to eat. Then the story went that he started killing campers at night, ripping their rib cages open! Terrifying but not believable.

Both Karl and Daniel were honor campers several times, which made Tom and me very proud. Each cabin chose one boy by secret vote, and the winners were called out at an Indian-style campfire ceremony.

"A counselor walked around the circle where all the boys were sitting on logs," Karl recalled. "He stopped behind each honor camper and pulled him up by the arm to stand and be recognized."

Indian campfires were a regular occurrence for different occasions. According to Karl, one of the biggest was the Indian tribal dance with a counselor playing the chief, telling Indian stories around the campfire. All the campers dressed in towel loincloths and feathers and any other adornments they could find or make. Raising his arms to the sky, the Chief called:

God of the North give us fire,
God of the South give us fire,
God of the East give us fire,
God of the West give us fire,
Let there be fire.

And magically a flame sprang up, helped by the Chief using his toes to pull a string in the grass tied to a bucket that emptied one chemical into another and started the fire. How that worked, I cannot imagine, and Karl said sometimes it did not.

Then two counselors dressed as warriors performed a ritual fight, swinging their torches at each other, leaping over the fire, and ending by running off together. The moral was: It is not who wins but the fight you put up.

When Karl and his friend Lyn Bruner were counselors, they performed a carefully choreographed and rehearsed battle. They greased their bodies with Vaseline as protection from the fire. Here is Karl's description:

"We went pretty all out. When it came time for me to jump over the fire, I took off on the wrong leg, my weaker leg, and barely skimmed the fire. Sparks flew up and singed my underside a little bit. Then Lyn and I clashed our torches and one piece of burlap flew off and stuck on my shoulder just as we were running off. All the kids were excited, and Tommy Martin, the new director who worried about everything, came flying to me.

"'Are you okay, are you okay?'

"I was fine. I had a little burn on my shoulder, but the Vaseline basically protected me."

Boys! Well, really men. Since Karl and Lyn rehearsed at our house, I was worried about the fire dance, just like Tommy, but did not witness the event and only heard about it later. Yes, bringing up boys can be scary.

Little did Tom and I know of the initiation ceremonies for first-year campers and honor campers. From what Karl and Daniel later told me, it got out of hand at times.

First-year campers were told that they would be taken up to the top of Friday Mountain, a 300 to 400-foot hill, blindfolded, put in a metal barrel, and rolled down the hill.

"It was terrifying," Karl said. "But I remember thinking Captain Kidd would not allow us to get hurt — that was my way of survival." And he was right. What really happened was that the boys were rolled around the top of the hill while older campers and counselors banged on the barrel with rocks. No rolling down the hill.

When I despaired after hearing about these rituals, Karl said, "Mom, it's what happens to boys." But I did not want it to happen to *my* boys.

The worst was initiation of the honor campers. One year when both Karl and Daniel were honor campers, all the boys had to chew a plug of tobacco and walk around with wet pillowcases on their heads, and every-one except Daniel got sick and threw up.

"None of that would be tolerated now," Daniel said years later.

When the tobacco incident came out, the camp changed policy, and a new director, Tommy Martin, was hired. Tommy had a PhD in psychology, and Karl described him as "an intelligent redneck." Instead of barrel rolls and chewing tobacco, he took the boys on a midnight walk and spoke to them about the importance of being a good person.

18

Boys of Summer

*C*aswell Tennis Courts played a part in our lives year round, but especially in the summer. The boys and I enjoyed tennis, they with friends and I with a group of women. Tom was not interested. Perhaps it reminded him of his boyhood frustration at losing to his father. He preferred to spend his leisure time sailing. Summers for him were like the rest of the year, except when we took family trips. He worked and supported our family like most fathers, while I took care of our boys and our home and worked at writing children's books. I loved our life.

When the boys were in school I rode my bicycle to Caswell on the Hike and Bike Trail on Tuesday and Thursday mornings and played with the Austin Women's Tennis Association. We occasionally had tournaments, which added to the competitive excitement. I always had trouble with my serve but loved playing at the net and occasionally slamming a ball down on the other side. Very satisfying.

Karl and later Daniel also rode their bicycles to Caswell, took lessons, and played tennis. Dressed in their whites, Karl and Bill Wilson made their way down the street to the Hike and Bike Trail just as they had once done on their tricycles.

It became a meeting place for O. Henry Junior High School students. Among the group that Karl played with was a bully, Jim Sayers, and his followers. Once he challenged Karl to a fight, and one of his followers stepped forward, not Jim, who was probably more bluff than brawn. While the others watched, Karl wrestled the boy to the ground, using Tom's techniques and winning the match.

Karl stood and said, "He winced."

Jim laughed in an attempt to save face. "He winced? What kind of word is that?"

Evidently not a word in his vocabulary.

But good times prevailed. Karl's friend Charles Larkam also played tennis at Caswell, and they entered tournaments together, one in Taylor, Texas, on the day camp started. I drove them to the tournament, and then Charles went along as I took Karl to camp a little late.

One day Daniel and his friend Gabe Thornhill were playing doubles in a Caswell tournament, and Tom came to watch after their game was already in progress. He walked across the court wearing nerdy shorts, shirt, and dark socks meant for long pants. I was watching from the bleachers and saw Daniel's chagrin.

"Who's that man?" Gabe asked Daniel.

Daniel just shrugged as if he had never seen him before.

Later, back at home, I was fixing lunch when Tom walked across our front yard.

"There's that man again," Gabe said.

Amused, I said, "That man is my husband, Gabe."

We all laughed.

At Tom's memorial Daniel said, "My dad was a spacey guy." Yes, he was, and it made him alternately lovable and irritating and funny, but mainly it made him Tom, a total original and all mine.

Summer was also a time for bicycle trips. In 1973 Tom and Karl embarked, or rather embiked, on a camping trip to Pedernales Falls State Park. We purchased bike bags that fit over the rear wheel for their supplies.

That summer morning when I saw Tom and Karl off in front of our home on Wooldridge Drive, I felt both happy that they were having a father-son trip and fearful for their safety on the road. Together we had mapped out a route by back roads to Wimberley, Blanco, and the

Pedernales, but they had to ride on Highway 290 for some distance to get to the park entrance. That worried me. There were no cell phones then, so I just had to rely on Tom and Karl to keep themselves safe.

The first night they stayed on Buck Winn's ranch near Wimberley. Buck, artist and inventor, and his wife Kitty were part of the UT School of Architecture faculty community. They knew the Shefelmen were coming and welcomed them with Texas Hill Country hospitality.

The next day Tom and Karl cycled on to Blanco by a county road with lots of ups and downs and expansive views. In Blanco they spent the night in a campground on the river and swam in the cool, clear waters.

Then on to Pedernales Falls State Park off Highway 290. There they set up camp on the banks of the wide but shallow Pedernales and cooled their sweaty bodies in the river. That night after supper, raccoons approached the camp with eyes aglow in the firelight.

Sometimes I wonder if I had good sense as a parent. In 1974, when Daniel and his friends were only twelve years old, Nancy Newman, Mary Stephenson, Sheila Schwiff, and I let our sons ride their bikes to Bastrop State Park — alone! What were we thinking? Maybe that if the other mothers thought it was okay, then it must be. But it was not okay, and I am grateful that nothing awful happened, although something did happen that revealed our lack of judgment.

We mothers hauled the bikes out to a starting place on a back road to Bastrop. After hugs and lots of "be careful" advice, we watched them head off. As we stood there, a big truck went by and gave a wide berth to our little boys who were riding single file along the shoulder.

The boys arrived at the park safely and set up camp. The next morning a park ranger showed up.

"Where are your parents?"

"In Austin," they answered.

"You're here alone?"

"Yes."

"How old are you?"

"Twelve."

"Did you know you have to be eighteen to camp here unless you're with your family?"

"Oh."

"I could fine your parents, but since you didn't know the age limit, I'll let it go this time." He looked at each boy. "You're a brave bunch to spend the night out here alone. Now I want you to break camp, ride into town, and call your parents to come get you."

We did come for them, feeling guilty about our parental responsibility — all except for Mary who thought it was funny. At least our boys gained self-reliance and had an adventure they will never forget.

Karl and Charles took a bike trip together in the 1970s to Lake LBJ where his family owned property. They rode out Highway 290 to 71. The traffic then was not as heavy as now. Still, I worried — the plight of being a mother.

They set up camp on Charles' property and settled down for the night, the first night Charles had ever camped out.

A sound in the dark scared him.

"Don't worry, Charles, it's just some night creature," Karl said.

But Charles was not sure. So they rode into town, found a phone booth, and he called his mom, asking her to come get him. Beverley called me, amused, and we drove out together. Between Karl and Beverley, a family therapist, Charles became convinced that he was safe there and all was well. Beverley and I drove back happy that by staying, Charles would gain confidence and be proud of himself.

During the summer of 1974, when Karl was sixteen and Daniel twelve, our family went in two different directions, Karl to Germany and Tom, Daniel, and I to Mexico.

I learned about the Experiment in International Living from our neighbor, Mary Elizabeth Pincoffs, who sent her daughter to Europe on the program and highly recommended it. The purpose was to immerse high school students in another culture. Since I wanted our sons to be citizens of the world and not just Texas, I asked Karl if he was interested, and he liked the idea. It would be his first trip abroad.

We chose Japan but it turned out that he would have been the only boy in the group. So we switched to Germany, to the town of Bad Neuenahr on the Rhine, famous for its grapes and wine production.

A group of boys and girls were assigned to live in homes in the town and come together for meetings and trips. Before leaving for Germany, the group attended a two-week session of language and culture classes at Windham College in Putney, Vermont, while living in the college dormitory. There Karl met Jody, his first love, never to be forgotten.

In Bad Neuenahr Karl lived with the Tempel family, mother, father, son Heinz Gunter who was Karl's age, and two younger brothers. Only Heinz Gunter spoke English, and Karl's German was as good as it could be after two weeks of language immersion. Sometimes, he said, it became exhausting to struggle to communicate. So it helped to be part of a group of American high school students and travel about, especially when in love with one of them.

Karl with Tempel Family

One cultural difference that Karl enjoyed was the fact that German children customarily drank wine with their parents in moderation. Perhaps drinking *en famille* kept them from sneaking into parents' liquor cabinets and drinking in excess as some American kids did — even Karl and Daniel, as they told me later. Once Karl got drunk at a friend's house, tried to walk home but got sick in our neighbor's front yard.

By contrast, *Herr* Tempel took the whole family, including Karl, to the local winery where they all enjoyed tasting the wines along with other families.

When the group arrived back in New York, Karl called to ask if he could go home with Jody to Grand Rapids, Iowa, for a few days before returning to Austin. By that time we were back from Mexico. It was heartbreaking, but I understood his feelings because I was once sixteen and would rather be with my east Texas boyfriend, Don, than my parents. So Karl stayed.

Tom, Daniel, and I had an adventurous trip to Mexico. We rode the train to Mexico City. There we rented a bright yellow Volkswagen Bug and drove to Teotihuacan, the pre-Columbian ruins northeast of the city, famous for its two great pyramids. Daniel scrambled up the steps of the Pyramid of the Sun and stood on top, triumphant with his plastic raincoat billowing out like a cape.

Then it was south to Puebla. Our intention was to climb Popocatepetl, visible twenty-five miles south of the city. We rented crampons, ice axes, and poles, and the next day drove to the lodge at Tlamacas, which sits on the saddle between Popo and Ixtaccihuatl at 12,000 feet.

A large one-story stone building with pitched red metal roofs, it seemed a comfortable place to spend the night before our climb. There was a spacious dining room, private bedrooms, and shared bathrooms. But there were problems. First of all the altitude, which made Daniel sick. And second, the plumbing stopped working and toilets were stopped up. How did we manage?

Barely. We hardly slept, but by the next morning Daniel felt better so we started up Popo, even though later than we intended. In hindsight that decision seems foolish indeed, as we would discover. For one thing, the proper climbing season is winter and this was summer.

We followed the rocky trail, traversing up the mountain, stopping to rest along the way. Our intention was to stay in a hut at 14,700 feet overnight and climb to the 17,802-foot summit the next day. But when we reached the hut and Tom opened the door, the odor of urine and feces poured out.

"Ugh," Tom said as he slammed the door shut. "We can't stay here; we have to go down. It's too late to climb on."

What a shock after our experiences on Mount Rainier and Mount Washington. The condition of this hut, added to the overflowing toilets at the lodge, gave me negative feelings about Mexican alpine tradition.

Just then a small group of people appeared, coming from above.

"It's impossible," one said. "The snow is too deep — up to our hips."

"Yeah, we're not going to try it," Tom assured them.

As we descended, dark clouds suddenly moved in. Thunder and lightning threatened us as we hurried down the mountain, exposed to nature's fury. Daniel was crying out of fear.

"It's going to be all right, Daniel," I told him over and over again, though I was not sure.

But at last it was. We reached the lodge, where miraculously the plumbing had been fixed.

We did not make it to the top, but we got down alive! In a way, we proved to ourselves that we could do what we needed to do. At least El Popo did not erupt, which it did in April of 2015, a major eruption that swept away that dirty little hut.

Our next destination was Oaxaca and the pre-Columbian ruins of Monte Alban and Mitla nearby. Driving there in our VW Bug, we came upon soldiers armed with automatic rifles blocking the highway. Scary! *What do they want?* I wondered. *Are they bandits or military?* I noticed that one of them had a gun with a slightly curved barrel. *Strange.* They did not look like professional military so they must be bandits.

173

Popocatepetl

We slowed and stopped and Tom rolled down the window.

One of the men approached and said, *"Estamos buscando drogas."*

I had taken Spanish in high school and college and knew that *buscar* meant to search. And *drogas* sounded like drugs. So maybe they were legitimate soldiers.

He motioned us to get out of the car and we did. After a search, the soldier nodded, the others stepped to the side of the road and let us drive on. *Whew!*

In Oaxaca we stayed in a hotel just off the *Zócalo*, the charming main square, shaded by tall trees. The Gothic cathedral stands on one side and arched *portales* with balconies above line the other three. Sellers of local woven goods and pottery spread their wares under the trees and marimba groups played while people strolled or sat in sidewalk cafes. One could spend the whole time here, but the ruins were calling to us.

Our first excursion was to Monte Albán, once the Roman Forum of the Zapotec civilization and roughly contemporary. The Zapotecs scraped the top of the mountain into a flat surface and erected stone platforms with wide stairs leading up to the buildings. The platforms remain but not the buildings.

Ancient ruins have always fascinated me. I love trying to visualize a place as it once was. Some 20,000 inhabitants, who called themselves the Cloud People, lived here high above the Oaxaca Valley. Their civilization lasted for over a millennium.

I don't know how much of the history of the ruins Daniel absorbed, but he learned that there were advanced civilizations in America before the Europeans came. He always had eyes for arrowheads on our ranch, and on Monte Albán he found a small chip of obsidian. As Tom and I sat at the top of the steps gazing out at the great plaza, Daniel came running up to show us his treasure.

"Mom, Tom, look what I found! Can I keep it?"

Tom took it in his hand and turned it over. "I wish you could,

Daniel, but this is not our ranch, not even our country, and so anything you find is not ours to keep."

Daniel nodded and laid it on the steps.

The next day we drove to Mitla, some 25 miles southwest of Oaxaca. It was a religious center for the Zapotecs. The name Mitla means "place of the dead," and it was considered to be a gateway between the world of the living and the dead. Human beings yearn for that connection, the result being religion. As Will Durant said, "Without death there would be no religion."

A few of the buildings are better preserved than those at Monte Albán, especially the palace, which still has brilliant red paint on the geometric stone fretwork designs. Spanish invaders, at the order of the archbishop, destroyed others. The stones were then used to build the Church of San Pablo on top of the ruins of a temple. Thus the people of Mitla became Christian and the Zapotec civilization came to an end.

And so that long-ago summer came to an end, Karl came home, still pining for Jody, and school started.

Daniel and Mom at Monte Alban

19

Changes

The mid-1970s was a time of change for Austin schools, the beginning of desegregation. During the summer of 1972 the district announced the plan. They established Sixth Grade Centers where children from all over the city would be bused, and unfortunately this was the year Daniel entered sixth grade. The idea that he would not attend sixth grade at our beloved Casis Elementary was upsetting.

I remember talking to the superintendent, Jack Davidson, when we both attended parents' day at Friday Mountain Boys Camp that summer. I expressed my displeasure at the plan. He must have heard objections all summer but he patiently explained to me that the district was under pressure to desegregate, and this plan was the least disruptive.

Still, it was a jolt. Daniel's Sixth Grade Center was the old Baker Elementary in Hyde Park, built in 1911. Fortunately it was not far away, so Daniel and I found a safe route that he could take to school on his bicycle. His teacher was quite good and encouraged Daniel to take a lead among his classmates who were white, black, and Hispanic. He was dubbed Encyclopedia Brown, like the popular book character, for his wide knowledge, and he became good friends with a black boy whom he tutored.

The next year Daniel attended O. Henry Junior High, as Karl had done. There he found other changes as well.

"Mom, the girls are different now," he said when he came home from school on the first day. "They changed over the summer. They stand around in groups and giggle."

I don't remember what I said. Hopefully something like, *This, too, will pass, Daniel.*

And eventually it did.

Mr. Wiley, the stocky principal of O. Henry, always stood at a hall intersection outside his office, feet planted, arms folded across his chest, to make sure there were no fights. Even so, it happened occasionally. Desegregation was new, and both faculty and students were learning how to handle it.

With junior high came the advent of the popular crowd phenomenon, which has eternally plagued teenagers. I suffered the exclusion, too, and longed to be one of them. Entry into the group seems to require having parents who socialize, a certain amount of wealth, living in the right neighborhood, church membership, football stardom, physical attractiveness, and social confidence.

Though I was cute, I was shy. My parents socialized with SMU faculty, not country club members, and we lived in University Park, not Highland Park.

Like my parents, Tom and I socialized with the UT architectural faculty, were not wealthy, and lived on the wrong side of the tracks (as Karl jokingly put it). Though both Karl and Daniel are good-looking guys, they were on the swimming team, not the football team (thankfully). And we had a sailboat, not a motorboat and water skis.

It broke my heart that our sons *wanted* to be in the popular crowd but were not admitted. Yet from my own experience, I knew that the popular students bloomed in high school and then faded. Even though I tried to tell both boys this, it is hard to convince a high school student who is trying to find his place in the world. Of course, they had a group of friends of their own, as did I.

Not long ago when Karl's film, *Looking for the Jackalope,* screened at the Alamo Drafthouse, he made sure that his high school class knew about it. They came and packed the house. Karl reveled when three girls from the popular crowd flocked around him saying, "We're so proud of you, Karl!"

At O. Henry both boys loved Industrial Arts class with Mr. Gober. Karl said, "It's the only class where you *do* something." Recently he stopped by O. Henry and looked in the shop window. Nothing had changed. Thankfully some things don't.

Daniel was foreman because of his workshop experience with Tom. Once a black student socked him in the stomach for being bossy. Oh, the things that happen to boys, my boys, that I never anticipated and could not prevent.

On a gentler note, since Tom and I had piano lessons when we were growing up, I decided Karl and Daniel should too. Helen Elsass, a teacher who lived near Casis Elementary was recommended, so first Karl and then Daniel took lessons from her, beginning in elementary school and continuing into junior high. She taught small groups of three or four at a time. We moms sat in her living room and listened.

Some brought little needlepoint projects to work on. I decided to try my hand by doing a wall hanging. It was huge, something like three by six feet, my first and last needlepoint. Still, I loved the project, which was transferring the boys' childhood drawings to the canvas. Hardly a laptop sort of job. It far outlasted piano lessons. After stitching in the drawings, I asked Mother to do the background. Being a professional with a needle, she finished the job, and the tapestry has hung on the wall of our homes ever since.

Thanks to those piano lessons, when Karl was in the sixth grade at Casis and about to graduate, he joined a group of musician friends and rehearsed to give a concert at their class graduation party. He asked Mrs. Elsass to teach him to play the Beatles' "Let It Be," and she did. At the outdoor party there was a stage set up, and Karl played the song accompanied by the group. It was a big success. I was there with other moms and felt so proud.

Years later Karl, Ellen, and I were in Westminster's Solarium. Karl sat down at the piano and played and sang the song from memory. I was stunned that he remembered the notes and words. As he sang, I realized for the first time how profound those words are. *Let it be.* Yes, one has to accept the sadness that comes to all of us and let it be.

Karl took to piano lessons but he did not like to practice, especially right after school. He wanted to be playing tag football at O. Henry. When I pushed him to practice, he said, "Okay, Mom, I guess I'll just be a piano player instead of a football player."

That gave me pause, and we made a compromise because he ended up doing both.

As for Daniel, he wanted to change to cello lessons with the UT String Project, and he did so for about a year. Then he came to a decision and turned in his cello.

"Face it, Mom, I'm an artist," he said. And he was right. He loved drawing cartoons and became the O. Henry *Rolling Stone* newspaper cartoonist and later editor as well. At Austin High he became the cartoonist for the *Maroon* newspaper. One of his cartoons set off a furor with the PTA.

Driving to school one day, Daniel saw an injured squirrel lying in the street. He stopped, picked up the squirrel, and took it to the Austin Nature Center for care. Thus he was late arriving at school and given detention, which meant staying after school, even though he had saved a creature's life.

This experience inspired a cartoon showing Jesus wearing a crown of thorns and standing before the assistant principal's desk. The caption said, "I don't care why you were late. I'm giving you detention." The PTA objected to the depiction of Jesus and wanted the principal, Jackie McGee, to remove Daniel from the newspaper staff, but she stood behind him and freedom of the press! What a lady.

Karl and Daniel were not straight "A" students, and we did not push them to be. Tom and I both valued creativity more. But occasionally

Karl's grades bothered me. Strangely enough, Mrs. Stubbs, the art teacher at Austin High, temporarily snuffed out that creative urge with her critiques. Later, learning from that experience, Daniel enrolled in a graphic art class at Austin Community College that had an arrangement with the Austin High curriculum.

In his last two years at Austin High, Karl became enamored with biology lessons with Mrs. Cadwallader. So much so that he decided to be a pre-med student at Kenyon, which turned out to be horribly competitive to the point of students hiding books from each other. That was not for Karl. Thus he decided to change his major to art.

More changes were to come. As the years went by, the traffic on Lamar increased and the noise bothered me. I began to look for another place to make our home. On one of my walks around the neighborhood, I discovered an almost hidden piece of property where 32nd Street ends high above Shoal Creek and the Hike and Bike Trail. There was an abandoned peanut brittle house on an almost half-acre lot and a for sale sign that had been knocked over.

I was intrigued, called the realtor, and found out that the old house was the original dairy farmhouse before the Bryker Woods neighborhood grew up around it. The house was to be torn down and the property sold for $30,000. A lot of money.

Fortunately our home on Wooldridge Drive was paid for, so if we sold it we could use those funds as a down payment and get a loan to build a house that Tom would design. It was a painful decision, especially since Daniel did not want to move. Karl would soon be off to college and not as affected as Daniel by the change. Still, the idea of Tom designing our house and involving the whole family in the process was compelling.

And so we put our beloved old house, the place where the boys grew up, on the market. Sometimes I wonder how we could do so. When it sold, we moved to a rental house down the hill at 1012 Gaston Avenue.

"I wish we'd had a farewell ceremony," Karl said the day we moved.

Why didn't I think of that? Later, to assuage my guilt I made a picture book using the boys' drawings and many photographs about our life in that house. I named it *Farewell, Old House*. Miller Blueprint Company printed the book with layout help from Harmony Grogan, friend and former employee at Shefelman & Nix, Architects. I sent copies to Karl and Daniel as birthday gifts.

"It's the best thing you've ever written, Mom," Daniel said. "It made me cry."

And Karl's Ellen told him, "I wish I had a book like that."

We lived for nine months in the rental house on Gaston Avenue, while Tom designed our new home. I can still see him sitting in the downstairs sunroom at his drawing board.

Tom hired Donnie Huebner, a contractor he liked, to build it during the spring and summer of 1976. Karl had just graduated from Austin High, and after a trip to Germany with a friend, Ed, spent the remainder of the summer as one of the carpenters working for Donnie. With all its angles, the building was not easy to construct. Karl remembers seeing Donnie sitting atop the framework at a corner, scratching his head. But with Tom's supervision, the Big House went up and we moved in just before Christmas, 1976. The Little House would be built next.

Carpenter Karl

Tom wrote an article for the *Texas Architect* magazine titled "House of Words" about our process, and there were a lot of words to draw. Words like "big house" and "little house" and "compound" set the image of the home we wanted on our large heavily wooded site that overlooked Shoal Creek.

Inspired by the site map in *Winnie the Pooh*, I drew a simple plan of our site with rectangles for a big house and little house, and Tom took it from there, turning my rectangles into more interesting shapes with few ninety-degree angles.

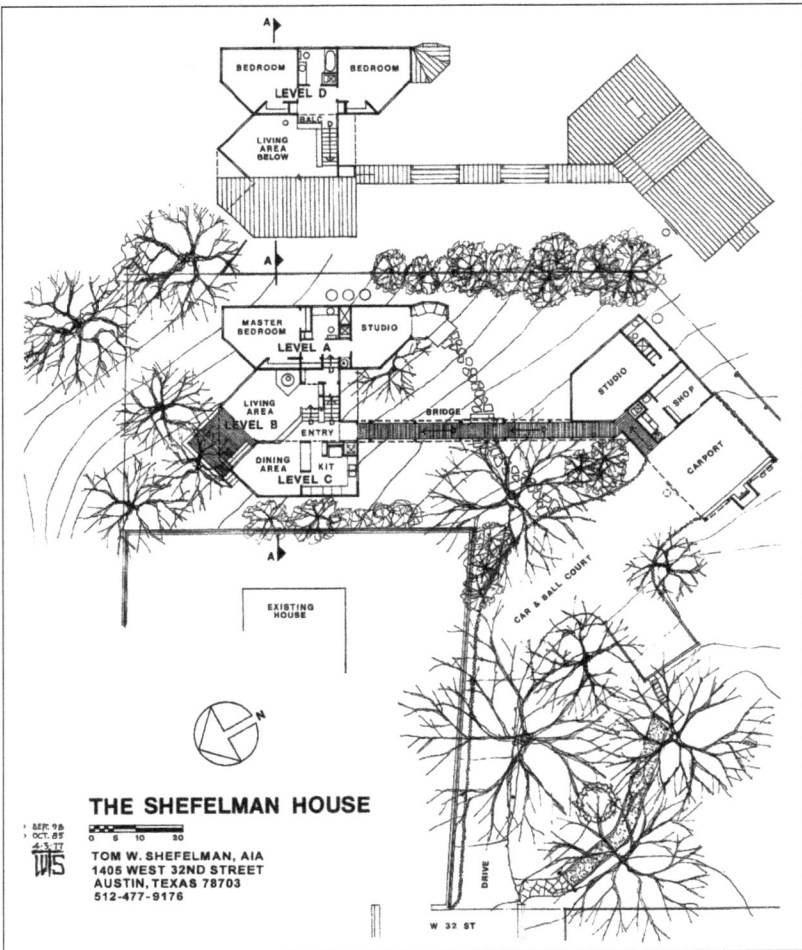

Shefelman House Plan

Though Tom had visualized a continuous and meandering urban house, he translated our words into a kind of rural compound of buildings made of cedar siding, set lightly on the landscape and connected by a bridge. The result was our *home* of words, which won an Austin Chapter AIA Award.

Daniel seemed to come around to accepting the change since we were still in walking distance of our old neighborhood but it was not easy. When his friend John first came to our new house and climbed down the cliff to the Hike and Bike Trail, he said to Daniel, "This isn't downbelowthecliff."

Nor did it help when Daniel, John, Reed, and Stuart built a hut in the bamboo patch at the far corner of our property, only to have it torn down by a nasty neighbor kid they knew. Still, Daniel did not give up.

Once, while our house was under construction, he and the same friends decided to spend the night on the framed platform where his upstairs bedroom would be. Perhaps it was a way of claiming the new house as his own. There were as yet no stairs. The boys had to climb up the framework.

During the dark of night, John's older brother, Wesley, snuck up and made noises, scaring the boys. Daniel clambered down and knocked on the door of our neighbors, the Von Biebersteins, whose house backed up to ours. They had been quite friendly, but Mr. Von Bieberstein did not open his door to the boys. In his defense I must say that his son was involved with drugs, which may have made his father wary of any knock on the back door in the middle of the night. No matter, the boys figured out who scared them, went back to their sleeping bags, and claimed the place.

And so high school days went by and college loomed with all the anxiety of applying and choosing. Karl decided on Kenyon on the recommendation of his swimming coach, who said the college had an excellent academic standing as well as swimming team and that the swimmers were "scholar athletes." The Kenyon coach, Jim Steen, offered an honorary scholarship, which did not mean financial assistance because such was not permitted in Division III. It just meant Coach Steen was eager to have Karl join the team.

Christmas in Our New House

At this crucial time when Tom and I were faced not only with the expense of college tuition but also paying off a house loan, TSVM disbanded. Taniguchi left the firm, as did Vackar and Minter. That only left Tom and employees, who mostly scattered. Very scary. But you do what must be done. It helped that TSVM had purchased their office building at 3rd and Congress, though I don't think it was paid off yet. It sold and brought in some money for us to make the transition.

We managed to get through the financial crisis by being frugal. Sometimes I was late paying a utility bill. Once when Mother was visiting us in our old house, someone came to collect.

Mother was aghast. "Why haven't you paid the bill?"

"Because we didn't have the money when it was due," I told her. "But now we do."

"I couldn't live like that," she said.

You never had to, I thought.

I decided to enroll in the UT Graduate School of Library Science so I could get a job in an Austin school. I had always loved working in elementary school libraries. My favorite course was children's literature, taught by Dr. Luckinbill. I began to think I, too, could write for children. Since my favorite kind of book to read was historical fiction, I planned a novel based on my German ancestors' immigration to Texas in 1845 and launched into research, much aided by Daddy's book, *Ernst and Lisette Jordan: German Pioneers in Texas.* The thrill of making the past and my ancestors come alive took hold, and I spent two years writing *A Paradise Called Texas.*

For his part, Tom asked Jim Nix, an employee of TSVM, to partner with him, and they started a new firm. They rented office space in the Perry Brooks Building, which Tom designed and where he began his architectural career with Kuehne Brooks and Barr.

After a year at UT, I received my library certificate and interviewed at several Austin elementary schools to no avail. Meanwhile I began substituting for librarians in Austin schools. It was sporadic and not rewarding, except financially.

Our Home, a Painting by Tom

188

In September of 1976, Tom, Karl, and I drove to Kenyon by way of the Smoky Mountains. It was a lovely trip but sad to think of Karl leaving home. We got him settled in his dorm room before his unknown roommate arrived. I was glad that Karl got to choose which bed he wanted. The only problem was that he did not get to choose his roommate, who turned out to be not so nice. Of course, we didn't know that at the time.

It was so hard to leave Karl there amid strangers. Sure, he had a ready-made group of friends on the swimming team and an extraordinary coach. Still ... I'm haunted by the sight of him standing alone as we drove away.

Karl's First Day at Kenyon

Back in Austin, I learned that Lake Travis Elementary was looking for a librarian for the fall. The new principal, Aggie Hall, interviewed me. Tom and I knew her from the Austin Sailing Club. Aggie wanted to make some changes and have an open schedule library as opposed to each class having a time to come while their teacher had a free period. This idea was encouraged in library school, so I was eager to implement it and got the job.

The Lake Travis teachers were resisting the change. Aggie later said she hired me because she liked my assertiveness and believed I could overcome the opposition. And I did because it was something I believed in as well.

Four years later Daniel followed big brother to Kenyon. Since I was a full-time librarian at Lake Travis, Tom drove Daniel and his belongings to Kenyon without me. Daniel also joined the swimming team, but instead of art he chose to major in political science and draw cartoons for the *Kenyon Collegian*.

Now bringing up boys was over, and even though I wanted it to go on forever, I had to let it be. It helped that I had a job I loved and that I was working on my first novel, which gave me a new purpose in life.

So, farewell boys of my heart, and hello men of the world.

Daniel's Room at Kenyon

About the Author and Family

After the boys left home, Janice went back to school and became a librarian at Lake Travis Elementary. She also began to write books for children. With the success of her first, *A Paradise Called Texas*, a Texas Bluebonnet Award Nominee, she turned to full-time writing. In his spare time Tom illustrated their books, among them *I, Vivaldi*, a picture book biography that received an International Reading Association Children's Choices Award.

The boys, now men, moved to New York where they follow their father's artistic career as filmmakers. Karl is a storyboard artist and wrote and directed his first feature film, *Looking for the Jackalope*. Daniel has worked on many animated films such as *Ice Age* and is a professor of animation and illustration at the Fashion Institute of Technology. Karl married Ellen Goldfader, and Daniel married Jane Reiss. Daniel and Jane have two children, Lena and Will.

www.ingramcontent.com/pod-product-compliance
Lightning Source LLC
Chambersburg PA
CBHW041829090426
42811CB00038B/2366/J